THE METAPHYSICS OF SCIENTIFIC REALISM

Also by Brian Ellis and published by
McGill-Queen's University Press

The Philosophy of Nature: A Guide to the New Essentialism

THE METAPHYSICS OF
SCIENTIFIC REALISM

Brian Ellis

McGill-Queen's University Press
Montreal & Kingston • Ithaca

© Brian Ellis, 2009

ISBN: 978-0-7735-3696-8   (bound)
ISBN: 978-0-7735-3699-9   (pbk.)

Legal deposit first quarter 2010
Bibliothèque nationale du Québec

Published simultaneously outside North America
by Acumen Publishing Limited

Library and Archives Canada Cataloguing in Publication

Ellis, B. D. (Brian David), 1929-
   The metaphysics of scientific realism / Brian Ellis.

Includes bibliographical references and index.
ISBN 978-0-7735-3696-8 (bound).--ISBN 978-0-7735-3699-9 (pbk.)

   1. Realism. 2. Science--Philosophy. 3. Metaphysics. I. Title.

Q175.32.R42E45 2010   501   C2009-905246-6

Typeset in Warnock Pro.
Printed in the UK by Cromwell Press Group, Trowbridge, Wiltshire.

To Jack Smart, teacher, friend and colleague

CONTENTS

PREFACE

This book began life as a series of occasional essays on the metaphysics of science, free will and the theory of moral obligation, but I think it has grown into something more than that, for it has a consistent and developing theme. I did not realize this at first. I was just doing what I love doing, and have been doing a lot since I retired from university teaching, namely, writing philosophy for my own enjoyment. But, one day, after re-reading an old paper of mine, it occurred to me that what I had written involved the systematic development of some of the ideas contained in this early paper, and their rational deployment in other areas of philosophy.

After I retired, I had many projects to complete; other philosophers saw to that. One was to write a substantial piece for the forthcoming *Companion to the History of Philosophy in Australasia* (edited by Graham Oppy *et al.*) The editors wanted me to write about my early work as a conventionalist in the philosophy of science, and the events that led me to reject conventionalism in favour of scientific realism. This project suited me. It was nicely reflective, and was one that I could easily complete without much need to go beyond the resources readily available to me in my own library. The first chapter of this book derives from this project.

The project also gave me occasion to re-read some of my old papers, including the one to which I have already referred. This paper, which I had not seen for over twenty years, entitled "The Ontology of Scientific Realism" was written in 1987 for a volume of essays in honour of Jack Smart. It reviewed the status of the theory of scientific realism, of which Jack was one of the founding fathers, and argued that this theory needed a great deal more work. It would have to be augmented in a number of ways, I argued, if it were ever to achieve its full potential. Without my being consciously aware of it, this paper also seems to have set the agenda for much of my philosophical work in the period since then. For, when I re-read the paper, I was surprised by what I found. It strikingly anticipated a number of the moves that I made later, which, at the time, I thought were new and innovative. This paper is reproduced, more or less as I wrote it, as Chapter 2 of this book. I am grateful to the publishers, Wiley-Blackwell, for permission to reproduce this material.

The rest of the book is concerned with the resulting development of realist theory. It contains a number of essays that I wrote without much awareness that they were linked. Certainly, they were not written with any overall structure in mind. In writing these essays, I was just doing what I love to do anyway: investigating philosophical issues that seemed to me to be important. This way of working was not really a break with the past, for this is how I have always worked professionally. I did not react much to the literature. I mainly worked on problems that arose out of my own work, and tried to reach my own conclusions. The advantage of this approach was that it made me proactive philosophically. The disadvantage was that I always had to search the literature after the event to find out what others had said about the issues being discussed, and then work hard to connect it to the literature, and take proper account of it.

In my present circumstances, I do not really have the resources to do this kind of scholarly research for the present volume. But, fortunately, this is not a book that can easily be seen to be heavily dependent on the work of others. Nor is it one that has been written in reaction to any such works. It is a book that depends almost entirely on the work that I have done myself over many years as a professional philosopher working on metaphysics and the philosophy of science. And, as far as I am aware, it is all, unless otherwise acknowledged, original stuff. It has been written mainly by drawing on my own past research, and in order to address my own dissatisfactions with that research.

I am grateful, first and foremost, to Jack Smart, who taught me how to think for myself philosophically, and originally defined scientific realism. I am grateful to all those, far too many to name, who have contributed to my philosophical education over the years. I am especially grateful to those who have read drafts, worked on, or responded to the papers included in this book – particularly to John Bigelow, John Fox, Behan McCullagh, Robert Young, Brian Scarlett, Alice Drewery, Stathis Psillos, David Armstrong, Stephen Ames, Adrian Flitney, Howard Sankey, Alexander Bird, Graham Nerlich, Colin Mitchell, Elaine Miller, Manfred von Thun, and Toby Handfield. Finally, thank you Jenny for keeping me connected to the real world.

Brian Ellis

INTRODUCTION

The aim of this book is to develop the metaphysics of scientific realism to the point where it begins to take on the characteristics of a first philosophy, that is, as a theory of the nature of reality that can reasonably adjudicate between theories in any field of enquiry that makes assumptions about what there is in the real world. As most people understand it, scientific realism is not yet such a theory. Nevertheless, the original arguments that led to scientific realism may be deployed more widely than they were originally to fill out a more complete picture of what there is. This picture is still neither clear nor comprehensive enough to be accepted as definitive. It is not clear enough, because there is an ongoing dispute about what kinds of properties or relations there must be supposed to be in the world, and it is not at present comprehensive enough to deal with quantum mechanics, non-locality or the phenomena of temporal passage. But if, as I believe, these and a few other important problems can all be dealt with satisfactorily, perhaps the ontology of scientific realism can at last be seen as a plausible candidate for the role of first philosophy.

In Chapter 1, I discuss the relationship between science and metaphysics. This chapter draws heavily on my own history as a philosopher of science working on metaphysical issues. I have included it here because the relationship between science and metaphysics is central to the issues being discussed. Also, I thought it might help some philosophers of science to understand the book better if they knew where I was coming from, and why I eventually turned my back on the kind of internal realism that I defended in the 1980s. In *Truth and Objectivity*, which was published in 1990, I made a concerted effort to defend internal realism. But I now think that this attempt failed. For I no longer think that there is a univocal theory of truth. The evaluative theory of truth that I had used to construct the foundations of logic developed in *Rational Belief Systems* (1979) was required for this purpose. But it is not the only theory of truth that is needed. For a theory of reality, we need to understand how our best scientific theories relate to the world. And the evaluative theory of truth does not tell us that. Theories of reality always depend on the basic metaphysical hypothesis that truth supervenes on being. So, what is needed for ontology is fairly clearly some kind of correspondence theory of truth.

Chapter 2 is the paper I mentioned in the Preface, which I had almost forgotten about. It is reproduced here in more or less its original form. The paper says quite a lot about the kind of thinking that led me to write some of the later chapters.

In Chapter 3, I outline the position of scientific essentialism, which was my first serious attempt to develop an adequate metaphysics of scientific realism. I consider some of the criticisms that have been made of it, and suggest some ways in which I should now be willing to change it. Most of the criticisms that have been made are, I think, wide of the mark. But there is one that requires much more attention than I have given it. This is the need for me to insist on the existence of a class of categorical properties distinct from that of causal powers. This is a contentious issue, for there is now a growing body of opinion that all properties are causal powers. I explain briefly what this problem is in Chapter 3. But a more complete answer requires that I should first develop a more adequate theory of causal powers than I have done so far. I do this in Chapter 4, and return to consider the problem of categorical properties more thoroughly in Chapter 5.

In Chapter 4, I develop my metaphysics to include quantum mechanical realism. Quantum mechanics has always been the main obstacle to acceptance of scientific realism, and hence to any metaphysics based on scientific realism. The difficulties lie with the de Broglie–Schrödinger theory of energy transfer processes. The proposed mechanism for this, the Schrödinger wave,[1] just does not look real. The particle emission and absorption events seem real enough. But the wave itself spreads out in all directions from the point of emission, and then, it seems, suddenly collapses at the point of absorption. The wave is unobservable during transit, and its amplitude must be interpreted as a sort of "realization potential". It is a theory that seems almost tailor-made to support scientific instrumentalism. But, however improbable Schrödinger wave realism may seem to be, I do not see that a scientific realist has any option but to accept this description of the process more or less at face value. Erwin Schrödinger's theory of particle transmission is one of the most successful theories in all physics, and the proposed mechanism for this process has to be respected.

Acceptance of Schrödinger wave realism has immediate and important consequences. First, it seriously undermines the argument for the temporal reversibility of all of nature's basic processes. The so-called "T-symmetry thesis" – the thesis that the fundamental laws of nature are all time symmetrical – still holds. For this is just the claim that $-t$ can be uniformly substituted for t throughout these laws, without changing their import. But the collapse of a Schrödinger wave (or, equivalently, the realization of just one of the many superimposed states that compose it) is almost certainly instantaneous, and therefore not subject to such laws. One cannot substitute $-t$ for t in a law of particle absorption that does not have t as a variable. Schrödinger's wave equation is itself T-symmetric. We know that. But there is no such thing as the instantaneous reflation of a Schrödinger wave. Hence, we also know that the absorption process is not T-reversible. Secondly, acceptance of Schrödinger wave realism forces us to recognize that there are two fundamentally different kinds of processes occurring in nature: energy transmission processes and instantaneous changes of state. Thirdly, it implies that Albert Einstein's theories of relativity have limited scope. Instead of being, as they are usually supposed to be, global theories, they must be just theories of energy transmission, and hence valid for only one of the two fundamentally different natural kinds of changes that can

---

1. I use the term "Schrödinger wave" not to give credit to Erwin Schrödinger for the wave theory, but to dissociate myself from Louis de Broglie's "guiding wave" interpretation of it.

occur in the world. Fourthly, it allows us to develop a physically realistic theory of the basic causal mechanisms in nature, and hence to say what is essentially involved in all physical causal interactions.

In Chapter 5, I return to consider more carefully the problem of categorical properties. My position is that categorical properties and causal powers are essentially different, and therefore members of distinct natural kinds. But to facilitate discussion of them, I introduce the concept of a dimension, which is, roughly, a respect in which things may be either the same or different.[2] Dimensions are demonstrably more fundamental than universals, and deserve to be recognized as primitives in ontological theory. What are classically called "universals" are, in fact, just the specific values of the dimensions, and therefore of little interest in themselves. Moreover, they are clearly dependent ontologically on the dimensions of which they are the specific values. Dimensions are important, I argue, not only because they are more fundamental ontologically, but also because, if we focus exclusively on the universals involved in any specific instance of a cause–effect relationship, we are likely to overlook the dimensionality of that relationship. To understand how categorical properties can have causal roles without themselves being causal powers, we have to understand the nature of this dimensional relationship. The categorical properties, I shall argue, are not themselves causal powers, but are essentially involved in the laws of action of the powers. For these laws of action are really just functions from the causal to the effectual categorical states of physical systems they relate.

In Chapter 6, I defend the idea that the metaphysics of scientific realism deserves to be accepted as a first philosophy. By a first philosophy, I mean a theory about the nature of reality that can plausibly serve to adjudicate on theories in other fields of enquiry in which assumptions are made about the basic nature of the world. For example, it would rule out any theories that depend on the truth of Cartesian dualism, because such an ontological dualism is clearly incompatible with the metaphysics of science. Yet such theories certainly do exist in other fields. For example, the theory of deliberative determinism that is defended by some libertarian philosophers

---

2. See Chapter 5 for a more formal definition.

implies that we human beings have the power to make deliberative decisions, which, at the time of making them, were neither causally determined nor a merely possible outcome of a quantum mechanically indeterminate process. The metaphysics of scientific realism rules out these possibilities. Therefore, anyone who accepts this view of reality must reject any form of libertarianism that is so defined. Extraordinarily, there is still a remnant of ontological dualism in some current theories of space and time. In particular, it is argued that temporal passage is an illusion owing to the fact that our perspective on the world changes with time. As time goes by, it is said, we view the world from different positions on our world-lines. But who, or what, is "we" in this context?

In the final chapter, I consider the implications of the metaphysics of realism for other aspects of moral theory. In particular, I argue that the theory not only requires the rejection of deliberative determinism, but also has implications for most other key ethical concepts, including those of moral responsibility, moral powers, moral rights and moral obligations. The required moral theory must therefore be radically different from any standard one. Some philosophers have tried to develop what they call "moral realism". But such theories require realism about moral properties, such as goodness, rightness, kindness, cruelty and so on. But these are not physical properties, as they are understood here, and therefore contrary to the tenets of a metaphysics of scientific realism. To my knowledge, there is only one kind of moral theory that has any plausibility, which can survive the rejection of libertarianism, namely, one that conceives morals to be social ideals. In the last chapter, I outline such a theory, define the required concepts of morality and discuss its merits and difficulties. I call this theory "social contractual utilitarianism". For, according to the theory, a moral judgement is one about what the person making the judgement would ideally like to see as being the accepted social norm in their conception of an ideal society.

1

SCIENCE AND METAPHYSICS

Truth is said to be what corresponds to reality. If this is so, then truth must be one thing, and reality another. Metaphysics, as I understand it, is an enquiry into the nature of this supposed reality. Presumably, such an enquiry, if it is possible at all, must start with whatever knowledge of the world we think we have, and consider what implications it may have concerning the supposed reality that gives rise to it. In this chapter it will be argued that an enquiry into the metaphysical implications of science is certainly possible, but is not itself part of science. For science is limited in what it can tell us about reality. What is needed, it will be argued, is not more science, but the progressive development of higher and higher levels of explanation of the world that is revealed to us by science. For the aims of metaphysics are different from those of science, and the structures of metaphysical explanations are different from those of scientific explanations. Metaphysical explanations all proceed from the premise that truth supervenes on being. And the general question being asked is: how does it supervene? Scientific explanations make no such assumption, and scientific enquiries usually stop short of asking this question.

Science is not limited, as the early positivists believed it to be, to just describing what can be observed, and constructing theories that will enable scientists to make sound predictions concerning future observations. Scientists do construct realistic theories about things, and some of them should certainly be taken seriously as descriptive of what there is. But not all theories are like this, and what many of them tell us about reality is unclear. There are also good reasons to think that there are essential limitations to scientific knowledge of the world, and that there are important questions that arise out of science about the nature of reality that cannot be answered by further scientific enquiry. Answering these questions is what metaphysics is all about.

Science can, in principle, tell us what is objectively true. But it cannot tell us whether, or if so how, these truths supervene on reality. It could, perhaps, if we had a good and workable correspondence, or metaphysical, theory of truth. But there is no such theory that is adequate to bear this metaphysical burden. Bertrand Russell's correspondence theory does not do the job, for well-known reasons. And the much more highly developed semantic theory of truth cannot be taken seriously, even as a rough guide to metaphysics, unless you want to be a "possible worlds" realist. What is needed, I shall argue, is an enquiry into the truthmakers of science. And what will ultimately be needed is a theory of reality that will accommodate these truthmakers.

The truthmakers are the things, properties or states of affairs that exist in the world, independently of our knowledge or understanding of it, whose very existence necessitates everything that is objectively true about it. It is reasonable, therefore, to identify the task of metaphysics as being to identify the kinds of truthmakers there are for the various kinds of known truths about the world, and to construct an overall picture of reality that is adequate to accommodate them. As we shall see, truthmaking is different from entailing, because a truthmaker is never just another proposition. A truthmaker is an existent of some kind that necessitates the truth of whatever it supports.

In what follows, I shall give a personalized, and no doubt airbrushed, account of the reasoning that led me to these conclusions, and to embark on this project.

Scientific knowledge and its limitations

Science is limited by what scientists are able to do. In practice, it is restricted by lack of resources, failure to make the required observations and the intellectual limitations of scientists, and in other ways. But let us imagine a world in which all such limitations have been overcome, as if by magic, and let us call the theory of the natural world that science would ideally deliver in such a world "the scientific worldview". Then, plausibly, this worldview has some claim to be considered the true one: the one at which we should ultimately aim. For, by definition, this is the view of reality that would rationally be accepted on the basis of the best and most comprehensive set of observations that human beings could possibly make. Nevertheless, most philosophers would probably say that even this ideal scientific worldview might not be true. There might be parts of reality that we cannot ever know about. Or, we might, either by accident or design, be systematically deceived about the nature of reality. Or, perhaps, we are just not biologically programmed in the right sort of way to discover the nature of reality – even in ideal circumstances. We can, no doubt, discover by scientific investigation many of the things that we (i.e. we human beings) ought rationally to believe, and rule out a great many things that it would ultimately be irrational for us to believe. So, even if there are limits to what it is possible for scientists to discover, the aim of discovering all and only those things that it would, in ideal circumstances, be rational for us to believe about the world would seem to be a plausible objective of scientific enquiry.

For many years, I assumed that these doubts about the limits of science reflected badly on the correspondence, or metaphysical, theory of truth that gave rise to them. I thought that many philosophers were just pretentiously wanting to play God, or see the world through the eyes of God. Consequently, I accepted the pragmatist theory that identifies truth with what it would ideally be rational to believe, and called myself an "internal realist", as others before me have done. I embraced this position, because the empiricist in me identified science with scientific enquiry about the nature of reality. And, I did not believe that there was any other kind of rational enquiry that could take over where science left off, or that scientific knowledge about the world was essentially limited in any way; or, if it were, then these limitations were essentially human limitations that we, as human beings, could never overcome. There might be a theory of science, a logic of science or an enquiry into the language of science or into the various kinds of concepts employed in science. But these enquiries were not, I thought, continuations of the scientific quest to understand the nature of reality. They were just meta-scientific enquiries, that is, enquiries about the nature of scientific enquiry, which philosophers of science were at least as well equipped as anyone else to undertake. The idea that one could continue the enquiry into the nature of reality by rational means that were not essentially scientific was one that struck me as preposterous.

This stance was reinforced for me, first, by my conviction that an evaluative concept of truth was all that was required for logic. In *Rational Belief Systems* (1979), I demonstrated that the standard deductive logics, including all of the quantified, modal and conditional ones, could be founded adequately in a theory of rationality, without presupposing a semantic theory of truth, or assuming the existence of any world other than this one. All that one needed for the purpose were some more or less self-evident principles of rationality based on a conception of truth as epistemic rightness. Secondly, I was, at the time, convinced that science implied its own ontology. For, it seemed to me that one could not rationally accept the truth of any process theory in science without accepting the reality of the processes that it allegedly involved. This was the classic argument for scientific realism that Jack Smart had used to such good effect in his *Philosophy and Scientific Realism* (1963). And I thought then that one does not need to have a metaphysical theory of truth to accept it.

In retrospect, I now recognize that it was a mistake to reject the metaphysical concept of truth when I did. For I now see that there are important questions about the nature of reality that cannot, even in principle, be resolved by the methods of science. First, there are many statements that are apparently significant claims about what is true in the world, which have been, and still are, widely regarded as conventional. The claim that the one-way speed of light is the same in all directions is such a statement. Yet the special theory of relativity that is based on this claim is greatly superior to any alternative hypothesis. Non-standard versions of the special theory of relativity can certainly be constructed, but they are all very much more complex than the standard version, and all involve arbitrary asymmetries, not only in the laws of electromagnetic radiation, but also in the behaviour of slowly transported clocks (since standard clocks must be seen to be speeding up or slowing down, depending on their directions of motion).[3]

Therefore, if truth is, as I once defined it (1985: 169), just what has to be accepted as part of the best overall theory, and nothing more nor less, then the claim that the one-way speed of light is the same in all directions must be considered to be true. But, if it is true, then there is yet a further question that needs to be asked, although it is not one that can be answered by further scientific enquiry: what is it about reality that makes it true? And the answer you give to this can only depend on your metaphysics. If you believe in the Riemann/ Reichenbach thesis of the intrinsic metrical amorphousness of space and time, as Adolf Grünbaum (1973: 8–18) does, then you will deny that there is any truth of the matter. But if you believe in the isotropy of space from the perspective of every inertial system, then you must accept that there is a truth of the matter. For the standard version of the special theory of relativity is the only one that satisfies this metaphysical hypothesis.

In my dispute with the Pittsburgh panel (Ellis & Bowman 1967; Grünbaum et al. 1969; Ellis 1971), the metaphysical question concerning the nature of the reality reflected in the special theory of relativity was never explicitly discussed. Yet, in retrospect, it is now clear to me that this is what was at issue. Grünbaum et al. accepted the "metrical amorphousness" thesis, which they took to imply that there are no naturally preferred metrics, or kinds of metrics, of space or time. For them, a metric, that is, a way of measuring dates, time-intervals, positions, distances and so on, must depend ultimately on coordinative definitions, which, they argued, are always matters for human decision. Therefore, a metric has always to be imposed on

---

3. If slowly transported clocks are assumed to remain isochronous, then the laws of electromagnetic radiation will be found to be isotropic. Ole Rømer's method of measuring the speed of light is one that is based on the assumption that clocks (in this case, the clock that consists of Jupiter and its moons) remain isochronous as they are moved around slowly, relative to the speed of light. Accordingly, Rømer's method must be regarded as a way of measuring the one-way speed of light by means of slow clock transport. Empirically, the speed of light measured in this way is the same whatever the location of Jupiter over its twelve-year cycle, and so, presumably, it is the same in all directions.

space and time, not discovered of it. Indeed, they thought, nothing about the required metric could ever be discovered empirically, because there was no metric to discover. But I did not accept this. For I thought that a theory that did not postulate, unnecessarily, any spatial anisotropies, and led to what was clearly the simplest and best theory of space–time, was obviously the one that ought to be accepted. But I had no answer to, and did not think it was necessary to try to explain, what made it right metaphysically to believe in the independence of the one-way speed of light with direction. I could answer the epistemic question of rightness to believe, but I could not answer the metaphysical one. If Grünbaum *et al.* were right, then there could be no truthmaker for this proposition: so, even if it were true epistemically that the one-way speed of light is independent of direction, it would not be true metaphysically. I think now it is true both metaphysically and epistemically, but I do not expect the former to be an empirical discovery.

Secondly, I did not understand the full force of Smart's argument for scientific realism until the mid-1980s, when I was asked to write something for a book of essays in Smart's honour. I now think that Smart's original argument for scientific realism requires much more than a kind of scientific entity realism, which is the variety of scientific realism that I advocated earlier. If one accepts realism about causal processes in the established sciences, and hence about the theoretical entities involved in them, then, by parity of reasoning, one should also accept realism about the causal powers that give rise to these processes, and about the spatiotemporal and numerical relations between things that characterize these processes, or the circumstances in which they occur. Or, if one does not wish to accept all of these things, then one must at least have a satisfactory reductive account of them.

Thirdly, I became convinced that, despite their good intentions, philosophers of science had erected many barriers to understanding the nature of reality. The principle of the metrical amorphousness of space and time is just one example. There are many others. It was, for example, fairly generally supposed that science had to be squeezed somehow into the straitjacket of a language with the structure of first-order predicate calculus. These languages, they thought, were adequate for stating everything that could be stated of a factual nature about the world. Modal languages, and languages with counterfactual conditionals, were the languages of "second-grade" discourse (as W. V. Quine described them), and were to be avoided. I thought, however, that these were precisely the kinds of languages required for scientific discourse, and that if these were not fact-stating languages, then so much the worse for the metaphysical thesis that science was concerned only with fact-stating. I thought, for example, that many of the laws of nature were universal counterfactual conditionals, that is, conditionals of the form: "If anything were an X in conditions of the kind C, then X would do Y, unless something interfered with it". Others, I thought, were concerned with what is physically possible, or impossible, and so were stateable only in a modal language. Therefore, the requirements placed on acceptable analyses mostly seemed to me to be absurdly restrictive.

In the 1960s and 1970s, "possible worlds" semantics for modal and conditional languages were developed, and the requirement that science limit itself to fact-stating took on a whole new meaning. For the languages we could now use, and represent formally, were not limited in function to stating facts about what there is in the actual world. In these modal and conditional languages we could also state facts about what exists in any of the merely possible worlds, and say which of these possible worlds are accessible to which other worlds, and which are the "nearest" ones in which, say "p" is true. And, all of these worlds are, by definition, ones that could, in principle, be fully described in extensional, that is, fact-stating, languages: languages fit for "first-grade discourse". Thus, the metaphysical pretence that the discoveries of science are limited to stating the facts could still be maintained. But victory was surely achieved at a very considerable cost to scientific realism.

As one who sought to derive ontology from science, it seemed clear to me that there are not, and could not be, any good reasons to believe that there are any merely possible worlds. There might conceivably be good reasons to believe that there are inaccessible parts of the actual world. But David Lewis had no such reasons. In *Rational Belief Systems* I demonstrated that there is a viable, and scientifically much more acceptable, alternative to Lewis's theory, which is to develop the appropriate ideals of rational belief, and demonstrate that belief systems on languages that have connectives and operators of the kinds logicians are seeking to define are rational if and only if they are rationally coherent, given these ideals. This is what I thought any good scientist would seek to do. And it is precisely what I sought to do in my book. But philosophers had long rejected this approach as "psychologistic". And, "psychologism", as nearly everyone knows, is a very dirty word. So, rather than try to come to terms with my approach, most philosophers just ignored it. In doing so, I contend, they deprived themselves of the only plausible explanation that anyone has ever been able to give of the usefulness of the fiction about "possible worlds" implicit in modal semantics.

To illustrate, if we wish to consider an ideally rational belief system that is as much like our own limited one as we can make it, but in which p is accepted as true, then we may easily do so, even if we ourselves believe that not-p. And, we may then use the theory of rational belief systems to determine whether q could rationally be denied in such a system. If not, then, according to the theory, the conditional "$p \Rightarrow q$" must rationally be accepted as true.

In general, to found a satisfactory propositional logic, or a predicate calculus, or to introduce modal operators and conditional connectives into a logical system, all one needs to do is develop appropriate axiom systems for rational belief systems on languages that have the relevant connectives and operators, and, effectively, to define them by the acceptability conditions for propositions that include them. Thus acceptability conditions can replace truth conditions in the foundations of logic, and ideally completed rational belief systems can replace possible worlds in the theories of modals and conditionals. And, the only price one has to pay for this is that one has to abandon the implausible Fregean idea that logic is the theory of truth preservation.

Where Gottlob Frege got this idea from is not entirely clear. But it seems to be implicit in the writings of René Descartes, who himself appears to have got it from Aristotle. In his *Posterior Analytics*, Aristotle distinguished two grades of knowledge, scientific and accidental. Accidental knowledge, he said, is knowledge gained by experience, that is, empirical knowledge. But for scientific knowledge, he said, we require knowledge of the cause on which a fact depends, "as the cause of that fact, and no other" (71b, 11). And, to have such knowledge, he said, we must have a demonstration of the fact from premises that are "true, primary, immediate, better known than, and known prior to, that which is to be demonstrated" (71b, 21–2). Descartes echoed this idea in the seventeenth century in his *Discourse on the Method of Rightly Directing One's Reason and of Seeking Truth in the Sciences*, commonly known by the abbreviated title *Discourse on Method*. To quote:

> Those long chains of perfectly simple and easy reasonings by means of which geometers are accustomed to carry out their most difficult demonstrations had led me to fancy that everything that can fall under human knowledge forms a similar sequence; and that so long as we avoid accepting as true what is not, and always preserve the right order for deduction of one thing from another, there can be nothing too remote to be reached in the end, or too well hidden to be discovered.
>
> ([1637] 1954: 21)

Plausibly, Frege had worked, as Aristotle and Descartes did much earlier, with mathematics as his model for scientific knowledge, and so imported into his theory the ancient idea that the primary aim of all deductive reasoning is to derive true conclusions from true premises. But whether this is so or not, the idea that arguing deductively is arguing in such a way as to preserve truth must have seemed very plausible at the time, as it has done to most philosophers ever since. Accordingly, the Fregean definition of deductive validity came to be almost universally accepted. An argument is deductively valid, Frege said, if and only if there is no interpretation of the non-logical terms of the argument in which the premises are true and the conclusion false. Or, as we now say, the argument is valid, if and only if there is no possible world in which the premises are true and the conclusion false.

But this did not seem to me to be a scientific approach to the study of logic. For logic was clearly concerned with sound reasoning, not truth preservation. Certainly, one would expect sound reasoning to preserve truth, if the premises of one's argument happened to be true. But why restrict logic to the analysis of such arguments? In developing the theory of rational belief systems, I approached the question of how people ought rationally to think about the world, as I imagined a scientist would. I was fully aware that ordinary human belief systems are incomplete, messy, confused and contradictory, and that human reasoning is often fallacious. Indeed, it is not just fallacious in random ways, but systematically so, as cognitive psychologists have convincingly shown. Nevertheless, I argued, there must be certain underlying patterns of human thought and reasoning that are universal. For, if this were not so, we should not be able to detect or identify cases of human irrationality as clearly as we can. Plausibly, I argued, these deep structures could be used to construct model-theoretic ideals of human rationality.

The resulting scientific theory is demonstrably one that enables us to develop epistemological foundations for all of the standard logical systems. So, as a theory, it was highly successful. Yet, despite the success of this project, I found myself becoming increasingly isolated philosophically. No one, to my knowledge, ever publicly acknowledged that the theory of rational belief systems provides an adequate foundation for standard logical theory. Nor was this thesis refuted in the literature, or even much criticized. Philosophers just went on believing in real but non-actual possible worlds, or that someone would some day tell them what these theoretical entities really are, without them having to abandon the idea that logic is the theory of truth preservation. The main influence that the theory of rational belief systems had in philosophy was just that it served as a springboard for the development of theories of the dynamics of belief. This was fine, but it was quite peripheral to what I was really aiming to do.

The case for metaphysics

Why was the Fregean conception of logic so sacrosanct? Why was there such resistance to founding logic in a theory of rationality in the same sort of way as Bruno De Finetti's theory of subjective probability theory is founded. The short answer is metaphysics. Truth just had to be a semantic relationship, it was thought, that is, a relationship between words and the world. And this was the theory of truth that nearly everyone believed a realist would have to accept. So, I just had to be wrong. Never mind that the theory that they thought had to be right led inexorably to "possible worlds" realism. Better to embrace possible worlds than a theory of truth that makes truth out to be nothing more than a mode of evaluation. Nevertheless, here I was defending the evaluative theory. I defended it (a) because the theory of rational belief systems clearly required such a concept, (b) because the pragmatic contradictions in "It is true, but I don't believe it" and "I believe it, but it isn't true" are best explained this way, and (c) because I could not see that anything would be lost if we were all to use such a conception of truth, and stopped worrying about whether we might all be just brains in vats, as Hilary Putnam once surmised.

Nevertheless, from the mid-1980s, I began to have serious doubts about the adequacy of the theory of truth that I had embraced. For it was, essentially, an intersubjectivist theory. If truth for me were just what I thought it was right for me to believe, then that would be purely subjectivist. But is the intersubjectivist theory that truth is what is true for us at the limit of our experience really much better? It might be better than the best we could ever hope to achieve through scientific enquiry. But it is still not an objective concept of the sort that (I now think rightly) is demanded by Australian realists.

In my book *Truth and Objectivity* (1990), I made a final attempt to rescue the theory of truth as a mode of evaluation, and hence to justify the concept of truth required for my analysis of rational belief systems. The consensus is that I failed in this attempt. And, in retrospect, I also think I failed. For I now think that there are two quite legitimate, but related, conceptions of truth with similar logics, just as there are two equally legitimate but related conceptions of probability (subjective and objective) that satisfy the axioms of the probability calculus. The subjective concept of probability and the evaluative concept of truth are the ones required for the evaluation of human belief systems, and hence for logic and scientific epistemology. The objective concepts of probability and truth are the ones required for talking about things that exist independently of human knowledge or understanding. That is, the objective concept of probability is the one required for the measurement of objective chances, and the objective concept of truth is the one required for metaphysics.

Consider John Fox's "truthmaker" axiom (1987: 189):

If p, some x exists such that x's existing necessitates p.

Or John Bigelow's supervenience thesis (*ibid*.: 205):

17

> There is no difference in what is true without a corresponding difference in the inventory of what is; that what there is determines what is true; that truth is supervenient on being.

These two theses are both intuitively very plausible. But neither is suggested, or even rendered plausible, by the theory of truth that I had been defending. For my evaluative theory of truth has no obvious implications concerning existence. It is, for example, as readily applicable to aesthetic judgements, or to the theorems of mathematics, as it is to the fundamental laws of physics. For example, to decide the question whether a given mathematical proposition is true, one only has to consider whether it has an adequate proof. One does not have to think about what exists in reality. If there is such a proof, then the proposition is true in my epistemic sense. No further argument. Whether, and if so how, it corresponds to reality are other matters.

In metaphysics, the focus is squarely on reality. And these other matters are now the ones that come to the fore. But the methodology of metaphysics is not that of science. It may start from science (or from anything else that we may think we know), and proceed from there. But the methodology of metaphysics is not that of science. It is not that of deriving consequences from one's hypotheses, and devising ways of testing them. Rather, it is that of arguing to the simplest explanation, without regard for testability. This was evident even in Smart's original presentation of the case for scientific realism. The best explanation of the continuing success of established scientific theories, he argued, is that the entities postulated in these theories really do exist. The causal processes described in these theories are not put forward just as "aids" to theory construction, as Pierre Duhem would have said. Nor are they considered to be no more than "analogies" of the kinds that should be required of any good theory, as Norman Campbell would have insisted. They are real, Smart said, and should be accepted as such.

Science, I would now argue, can tell us what we ought rationally to believe on the basis of our observations and experiments. But it cannot tell us what would make any belief of ours true in the required metaphysical sense. To do this, we need a good overall metaphysical theory, and a good ontological explanation of the truth of this belief, given that theory. The marks of such explanations are metaphysical necessitation and ontological plausibility. For metaphysical necessitation, the things or states of affairs that are postulated to exist must be such that, if they exist, then whatever truths are to be explained ontologically are necessitated by them. And for an ontological hypothesis to be acceptable, the things or states of affairs that are postulated to exist must be things that plausibly do exist, given our overall metaphysical theory.

Metaphysical necessitation is the relation that holds between things in the world and the things they make true. That is, it is what is usually called "a semantic relation". We need not be concerned at this point about what sorts of things these worldly objects are. One common view is that they are states of affairs (Armstrong 1997). But, as we shall see, there is reason to think that this answer is not entirely satisfactory. On a narrow understanding of "states of affairs", an ontology of states of affairs is one of atomic facts. But, plausibly, we need a much richer ontology than this to accommodate all of the kinds of things that our science leads us to believe in. The concept of plausibility that we require to define semantic relations all depend on our general metaphysics, that is, our theory of the ultimate nature of reality. And, for such a theory to be adequate, it must be consistent with our best understanding of the world, and able to accommodate all of the things we truly believe in. This is a logical circle, of course. But it is inescapable. A postulated existent is ontologically plausible if and only if it fits into an adequate metaphysical theory. And a metaphysical theory is adequate if and only if it accommodates all of the things that we truly believe in.

The fundamental importance of ontology

A necessitation relation is metaphysical if the proposition p whose truth is to be explained is made true by some objectively existing thing or state of affairs X. It is not enough that the proposition be entailed by other propositions that we happen to believe to be true. For the aim of a search for truthmakers is to show how the truth of a proposition might plausibly be supposed to be grounded in reality. It is not enough to show that what we believe to be true is something that we must believe, given our other beliefs, for this would only shift the problem to these other beliefs. "What would make them true?", we might ask. No, what we have to do is specify an X such that (a) X could plausibly exist, and (b), if X were to exist, then *p* would have to be true.

To make such a judgement, however, we must clearly have some idea of the sorts of things we are looking for. That is, we must have some prior views about the nature of reality. For it is only in relation to such a theory that we could possibly make a judgement of plausibility. So the question arises: what things or kinds of things should we suppose there to be in the real world? This question cannot be answered *a priori*. For such an answer would be either vacuous or culturally prejudiced. On the other hand, we cannot derive our ontology directly from science, because science does not answer the hard metaphysical questions. Our science may be able to tell us some things that are true about the world. But it cannot tell us what sort of world would be required to accommodate these truths. For example, we may ask "What sort of world would be required to accommodate quantum field theory?", or "What are the metaphysical implications of contemporary cosmological theories?".

In the introduction to his great paper of 1847 on the conservation of force (energy), Hermann von Helmholtz wrote:

> Science regards the phenomena of the exterior world according to two processes of abstraction: in the first place it looks upon them as simple existences, without regard to their actions upon our organs of sense or each other; in this aspect they are named matter. The existence of matter in itself is to us something tranquil and devoid of action: in it we distinguish merely the relations of space and of quantity (mass), which is assumed to be eternally unchangeable. To matter, thus regarded, we must not ascribe qualitative differences, for when we speak of different kinds of matter we refer to differences of action, that is, to differences in the forces of matter. Matter in itself can therefore partake of one change only, – a change which has reference to space, that is, motion. Natural objects are not, however, thus passive; in fact we come to a knowledge of their existence solely from their actions upon our organs of sense, and infer from these actions a something which acts. When, therefore, we wish

to make actual application of our idea of matter, we can only do it by means of a second abstraction, and ascribe to it properties which in the first case were excluded from our idea, namely the capability of producing effects, or, in other words, of exerting force.

([1847] 1935: 213–14)

In this passage, Helmholtz was outlining his overall theory of "the external world". This was straightforwardly a piece of metaphysics. It did not express his, or anyone else's, scientific conclusions about the nature of this world. For you could not possibly test the validity of his ontological abstractions. No, his metaphysical theory was not a scientific discovery. It was rather a framework for the introduction of his radically new theory of force (energy): one within which, he thought, his new theory of force (energy) would fit nicely.

In today's term's Helmholtz's ontology was one of material things with causal powers of various kinds, by which they both are known to us and affect each other. As such, it was a great advance on the ontologies that had been embraced in previous centuries, in which the external world was considered to be essentially passive (Ellis 2001). Helmholtz's external world was certainly not passive: on the contrary, it was essentially active. Nevertheless, Helmholtz's ontology is no longer acceptable. Mass can no longer be accepted as the measure of the quantity of matter. Nor can the internal mental world of human experience reasonably be separated from the external one of physical reality. Nor is Helmholtz's picture of the world as made up of discrete objects any longer appropriate. For modern theoretical physics is dominated by field theories, and their reality as physical existents cannot plausibly be questioned. However, no new ontology has been developed to replace Helmholtz's mid-nineteenth-century perspective. And what is needed urgently today is much more of the kind of abstract thinking that lay behind Helmholtz's theory of force. For our aim must be to arrive at a general theory of the nature of reality that can accommodate everything that we now believe to exist. I am not talking about what physicists would call "a theory of everything", which, like any other scientific theory, would be a testable one. I am talking about an abstract conception of the nature of reality that would make plausible the kinds of ontological reductions that we are seeking in our search for truthmakers.

In many cases, the required truthmakers are obvious. The proposition that a cat is on the mat, for example, is obviously necessitated by a cat being on the mat. And, provided that this is ontologically plausible, the proffered explanation must qualify as adequate. Propositions such as this may be said to be ontologically transparent. But in many cases, the truthmakers for what we believe to be true are much harder to find. In some cases, for example, the proposition seems to be saying something that is incompatible with our overall metaphysical theory. Propositions about our own thoughts and mental experiences, for example, do not sit easily with an overall physicalist ontology, and a good deal of work is required to explain how such propositions could plausibly be supposed to have physical truthmakers. In other cases, the trouble would sometimes appear to lie in the generally accepted semantic theory for propositions of the kind in question. For example, many people would say that "Not p, but possibly p" is true if and only if (a) "p" is false, and (b) there is a possible world that is "accessible" from this one in which "p" is true. But if one does not already embrace an ontology that includes merely possible worlds, then this would not be, or even suggest, what could plausibly be an adequate metaphysical explanation of the truth of the proposition in question.

The hard work of constructing satisfactory metaphysical explanations lies in developing a sound concept of ontological plausibility. For this is what is needed to determine the adequacy of any proposed truthmakers for the facts to be explained. In semantic analysis, as it is usually practised, the only constraints on any proposed interpretations of formal languages are that they should be adequate for logical theory. If a model allows the construction of consistency and completeness proofs, and the derived logics are of the kind being sought, then it might well be accepted as a satisfactory one. But, while this may be a good strategy for developing logical theories, the proposed models for interpreting formal languages should not be accepted automatically as springboards for constructing ontologies. A formally adequate semantics for a given area of discourse no doubt puts constraints on ontological theories concerned with this area. For any such theory must be able to explain why the models that have been accepted are as good as they are. But a sound ontological theory needs to be part of a broader theory that is adequate for the whole spectrum of human knowledge.

2

THE ONTOLOGY OF
SCIENTIFIC REALISM[1]

Scientific realists believe that an ontology adequate for science must include theoretical entities of various kinds, and that it is reasonable to accept such an ontology as the foundation for a general theory of what there is. J. J. C. Smart elaborated this doctrine in his *Philosophy and Scientific Realism* (1963). The theory he proposed was mainly about what really exists, that is, it had an *ontological* orientation. Theories with similar orientations have been defended recently by Nancy Cartwright (1983) and Michael Devitt (1984). The theory I called "scientific entity realism"[2] was also a theory of this kind. These theories may be contrasted with those semantically oriented versions

---

1. This chapter was written for a book of essays published in 1987 in honour of J. J. C. Smart, who was my teacher and mentor (P. Pettit, R. Sylvan & J. Norman [eds], *Metaphysics and Morality: Essays in Honour of J. J. C. Smart* [Oxford: Blackwell, 1987]). I reproduce it here more or less as it was written. I have made some stylistic changes to bring it into line with my current way of writing. But substantially it is almost exactly as I wrote it. The essay is important, because it did much to set the agenda for my philosophical work in the years since then.
2. Mentioned in my *Rational Belief Systems* (Oxford: Basil Blackwell, 1979), 45–6, and discussed briefly in "What Science Aims to Do", in *Images of Science: Essays on Realism and Empiricism, With a Reply by Bas C. Van Fraassen*, P. Churchland & C. Hooker (eds), 166–93 (Chicago, IL: University of Chicago Press, 1985).

of scientific realism that often seem to be more concerned with the theories of truth and reference than with what there is.

The ontology of scientific realism is supported by an argument from the best explanation: if the world behaves *as if* entities of the kinds postulated by science exist, then the best explanation of this fact is that they really do exist. Properly understood and used, this is a good and powerful argument. But there has been little attempt made to find out what its scope and limitations are; and scientific realists have generally presented it crudely as an argument for the existence of "things like atoms and electrons" – as if this were all that needed to be said. However, the argument is *not* a good argument for the existence of *some* kinds of theoretical entities (such as space–time points), and it *is* a good argument for the existence of certain kinds of properties and relationships that many scientific realists do not believe in.

The aims of this chapter are: (a) to discuss the scope and limitations of the main argument for scientific realism; (b) to spell out some more discriminating criteria for the existence of theoretical entities than this argument provides; and (c) to use these criteria to elaborate and defend a sophisticated realist ontology for science. I shall not, however, attempt to argue that this ontology is adequate as the foundation for a general theory of what there is.

Scientific realism

Scientific realism and descriptivism

Smart's original scientific realism was realism about certain kinds of theoretical entities, such as atoms and electrons. His opponents were the *instrumentalists*, who regarded the theories that postulated these things as just more or less powerful instruments for prediction, and the *logical positivists* who sought to reduce all talk about atoms, electrons and the like to talk about observables. It is not that Smart was opposed to ontological reduction. On the contrary, much of his book argues for the reduction of mental events to brain processes (Smart 1963). It was just that the attempts, particularly of the logical positivists, to construe the theoretical entities of science as logical constructions out of observables seemed to him to be entirely wrong-headed. The theoretical entities of science *explained* the world as we observed it, just as he thought the microprocesses of the brain would eventually explain our experience of it. Therefore, their existence must be ontologically more fundamental than our experience, and any ontological reduction must be in their direction. I think Smart was quite right about this.

Some more recent versions of scientific realism are: (a) the *successful achievement version*, that the laws and theories of the mature sciences are mostly approximately true; (b) the *goal-directive version*, that science aims to give us a literally true story of what the world is like; (c) the *semantic version*, that non-observational terms in scientific theories typically refer; and (d) the *descriptivist version*, that the theoretical statements of science are, or purport to be, true generalized descriptions of reality. In these versions of scientific realism, the issue is seen as being concerned directly with the referentiality of theoretical terms, or the truth or meaning of theoretical statements, and only indirectly with ontology. The four versions also have this in common: they all regard the laws and theories of science as more or less accurate, more or less general, descriptions of reality. They are all descriptivist theories.

By "descriptivism" I mean the views: (i) that the aim of science is to give a true, generalized description of reality; and (ii) that the laws and theories of science should be evaluated, as descriptions generally are, by their truthfulness, objectivity and economy. I think that this is wrong, both about the aim of science, and how scientific theories should be evaluated. The primary aim of science, I want to say, is to *explain* what happens, not just to describe it, or even to say what always, or usually, happens. It is true that some explanations are, and are intended to be, descriptive of underlying events or processes, or of general features of the world that the facts to be explained instantiate. But many explanations are not like these, and cannot plausibly be interpreted as descriptions of things. Accordingly, I think descriptivist criteria for evaluating theories are not always the most appropriate. In particular, they do not include what I think is the most important of all criteria for evaluating theories, namely their *explanatory power.*

However, there is no denying that many scientific theories were originally offered as descriptions of things or processes that are not directly observable. For example, the atomic and molecular theories of nineteenth-century chemistry, and the Bohr theory of the atom, were clearly intended to be taken literally as descriptions of unobservable physical structures and processes. The entities postulated in these theories were assumed to have certain properties, similar in some ways, but different in others, from the things we already know about, and to participate in various causal processes to give rise to the phenomena to be explained. I call such theories "causal process theories". For these theories, the usual arguments for realism concerning the entities postulated in them are mostly sound. However, to argue as though all, or nearly all, scientific theories are causal process theories, as some scientific realists seem to, is to show no awareness of the variety of aims of theory construction, of the diversity of kinds of theoretical entities in science, or of the different roles that scientific theories have. There are many important, indeed fundamental, theories that plainly are not intended to describe hidden structures or processes, and realism about the theoretical entities postulated in these theories may not be reasonable.

It is commonly assumed by scientific realists that a language without modalities or counterfactual conditionals should be adequate for science, perhaps because it is thought that such a language should be adequate for the descriptive purposes of science.[3] In fact, scientific laws and theories *are* often expressed in such a language. But the language of science may be somewhat misleading in this respect. The more basic sciences are at least as much concerned with *possibilities* as with actualities, and many of the terms they use do not name actual systems, or kinds of systems of which there are any real instances, but systems that are variously simplified or idealized. Many a paragraph in a physics text, for example, will begin by inviting us to consider some arbitrary system of such-and-such a kind (although it is clear from the context that there are no such systems), and end by formulating, in declarative language, some derivative law concerning its behaviour. Despite the language used, however, the terms occurring in these formulations typically do not refer.

---

3. Smart endorses Quine's position on this. See W. V. O. Quine, "The Scope and Language of Science", in his *Ways of Paradox and Other Essays*, 215–32 (New York: Random House, 1966), and J. J. C. Smart, *Between Science and Philosophy* (New York: Random House, 1968), 164.

This is not just a debating point. For science is fundamentally concerned to *explain* what happens in nature, not just to describe it. If Hempel's theory of explanation had been sound, then laws would be true generalizations about reality, and a descriptivist theory of science would be tenable, because explaining would then be just a matter of subsuming events under laws. But scientific explanations are not typically like this. To understand why an event or process occurs, we often need to know what contributions are made by various factors to its production; and this frequently involves having a knowledge of counterfactuals, and sometimes even of counterlegals. For what we need to know is what would happen in the absence of this or that factor, even if the factor is never, or cannot ever, be absent. It is essential to the task of science to develop the framework for such explanations, and many of the laws and theories of science, particularly of physics and cosmology, do just this.

Physical geometries, for example, may not, and probably should not, be construed as being descriptions of space or space–time. Their purpose does not appear to be descriptive of the actual world. Rather, their aim would seem to be to present a theory of the range of *possible* spatial or spatiotemporal relationships. In order to construct such theories, geometers have proceeded by postulating infinite sets of *possible* locations, or points in space or space–time, and then construed the actual world as consisting of things or events occupying various subsets of these sets of points. They have thus presupposed the existence of a world made up of objects or events precisely located in space, or space–time. However, the arguments for scientific realism do not present much of a case for interpreting these geometrical theories so realistically. First, physical things and events may not be precisely located, as geometrical realism would imply. Indeed, the argument for quantum mechanical realism would lead us to deny that precise physical locations exist. Therefore, the actual spatial or spatiotemporal relationships between objects or events may not be exactly like those postulated as holding between sets of geometrical points. Secondly, it is at least arguable whether physical geometries are, or are intended to be, causal explanatory theories. If not, then we may not need an ontology that includes infinitely many space or space–time points *in addition* to the physical entities, which we suppose may occupy them. If points in space or space–time have no causal explanatory roles, it is not clear how we can argue that the world behaves *as if* they existed.

Other theories appear to describe how certain *ideal* systems would behave in various specified circumstances, for instance in the absence of certain forces (which may never in fact be absent). Thus, the laws of conservation of energy and momentum apply strictly only to closed and isolated systems (although there are no macroscopic systems other than the universe as a whole that are like this, and whether these laws apply to the universe as a whole is at least problematic); the principles of special relativity tell us how things would behave in inertial systems (although general relativity implies that no such systems can exist); certain of the laws of thermodynamics apply only to perfectly reversible heat engines (which other principles of thermodynamics clearly prohibit).

Theories like this that cannot plausibly be interpreted realistically are not at all unusual. Yet the laws they contain are among the most fundamental in science. Therefore, they cannot be dismissed as anomalies. On the other hand, they cannot be taken to be true, generalized descriptions of nature either, for then the theories would all be vacuous. I think these fundamental laws and theories, which apparently refer to idealized systems of various kinds, which we know on other grounds could not possibly exist, have to be understood as *framework principles*.

Framework principles have been discussed extensively in the literature; so I shall be brief. The best-known example of such a principle is Isaac Newton's law of inertia. This law is clearly not just a vacuously true generalization about how bodies not subject to the action of forces actually move. If it were, it would be of no conceivable interest. Its role is not to *describe* the motions of things as we find them, but rather to provide a framework for *explaining* them. It does this by setting up an ideal of force-free motion with which the actual motions of things may be compared, and so partly explained. The part of the motion that is considered to be force-free is explained by subsumption under the law of inertia. And, what remains to be explained is the *difference* between this motion and the motion that actually occurs. In the context, this difference is the *effect* that requires causal explanation. Now the laws of conservation of energy and momentum, the principles of special relativity and some of the laws of thermodynamics all have roles similar to that of the law of inertia. They do not themselves offer causal explanations of events. But they do serve to identify and gauge the effects that need such explanations. That being the case, there may be no good argument from the best explanation for the existence of *any* of the theoretical entities postulated in these theories.

These points about the variety of kinds of laws and theories in science, and the inability of descriptivist theories to deal with the full range of cases, are well known and widely accepted. Yet many descriptivists are inclined to be dismissive of this criticism, and insist on regarding the laws and theories for which their account fails as just more or less crude approximations of the truth. They envisage that these laws and theories will eventually be replaced by *better* ones that will *more accurately* describe reality. The case of Boyle's law being replaced by van der Waals's equation is often cited as an example of such progress. But Boyle's law has not been replaced by van der Waals' equation of state, and the modified law is better only in the sense that it gives a more accurate account of the behaviour of real gases. From the point of view of physical theory, *Boyle's law is still the more fundamental one*, because it defines the standard with which real gases are to be compared, and their characteristic ways of behaving are to be measured and explained. In general, the more fundamental law or theory is not necessarily that which is descriptively the more accurate, and modifications of fundamental laws designed merely to increase their descriptive accuracy are, in themselves, of little scientific interest.

The point can also be made with regard to laws that apply strictly only in certain ideal situations. Galileo's laws of projectile motion, for example, tells us how things would move in inertial systems in uniform gravitational fields without air resistance. Yet Galileo's laws are still theoretically important. The corrections we need to make because the earth's gravitational field is not uniform, because the earth is not an inertial system, or because there is air resistance, are theoretically unimportant. Of course, if we wish to apply physical theory to solve practical problems, we must know how real things behave in practice. Industrial or military engineers who want to predict the behaviour of real gases or projectiles must know how to modify the fundamental laws appropriately. *But science is not engineering*, and it is a mistake to try to evaluate scientific laws and theories by criteria that are more appropriate to engineering than to science.

Boyle's law and Galileo's laws of projectile motion are admittedly not very fundamental. So the view that these laws are just approximations to the truth, which will eventually be replaced by laws that are descriptively more accurate, may have some force. But the more fundamental laws of Newtonian mechanics from which they may be derived (in the case of Boyle's law, the kinetic theory of gases) by making some simplifying assumptions apply strictly only to *point masses* moving under the influence of forces in *inertial systems*. So they too idealize reality. Hence, if these more fundamental laws are to be evaluated by descriptivist criteria, they will also be found wanting. It is true that Newton's laws of motion have been replaced by those of the special theory of relativity, and that Einstein's laws yield more accurate predictions, detectably so where high velocities are involved. But Einstein's theory is not just a modification of Newton's that has been made in the interest of greater realism, as Johannes Diderik van der Waals' modification of Boyle's law was. It is a radically different theory that idealizes reality no less than Newton's. It is valued, not just because it yields more accurate predictions than Newton's theory, which it does, or because the entities it apparently refers to are more realistic, which they are not, but because it explains the Lorentz invariance of Maxwell's equations, which Newton's theory was unable to do. In all this, there is no evidence of a trend to greater realism concerning postulated theoretical entities. Point masses and inertial systems are no more realistic in special relativity than in Newtonian mechanics.

The main argument for scientific realism

The most important argument for scientific realism is an argument from the best explanation. It would be "too much of a coincidence to be believed", Smart claimed (1963: 47), if the world were to behave just *as if* the entities seriously postulated by science existed, if they did not really do so. This argument for the existence of the theoretical entities of causal process theories is always a good argument. If A is agreed to be the best causal account that can be given of the occurrence of some event E, and A is a satisfactory theory, then the entities postulated in A as the *causes* of E must also be thought to exist. To say that it is just *as if* they existed is always to weaken the explanation, for it immediately raises the further question why this should be so; and the realist answer, "because they *do* exist", appears to be the only satisfactory one. We should, therefore, always be realists about the theoretical entities postulated in the causal process theories we accept.

This argument, which is the main one for scientific realism, applies strictly only to the theoretical entities of *causal process theories*. For it gains its strength from the roles these entities are supposed to have in bringing about what is to be explained. The world has to be *as if* these things existed. This is why the argument is a good one for the existence of things like atoms and electrons, as its proponents claim. However, there are other kinds of theories in which there are theoretical entities that are not supposed to have any such causal roles, and the argument simply does not apply to them. Therefore, it is not a strong argument for any form of scientific realism that does not distinguish between different kinds of theoretical entities. It is not even a convincing argument for wholesale realism about those entities that are postulated as causes in the causal process theories we accept. As the so-called paradox of the preface shows, "each" does not epistemically imply "all". Scientific realists may therefore concede that probably some of the entities they believe in do not exist.

To determine the scope of the main argument for scientific realism, we must distinguish clearly between those entities that are supposed to be involved in causal processes and those that are not. I do not know precisely how to do this, but one distinguishing mark appears to be that they should have effects other than those they were introduced or defined as having. The point derives from James Clerk Maxwell, who held that a quantity must be related to other quantities, independently of how it is defined, if it is to count as a genuine physical magnitude. Otherwise, he said, it is a "mere scientific concept". Maxwell made this distinction in the course of a discussion of Lord Kelvin's analogy between the laws of electrostatics, and those of heat conduction (Maxwell 1881: paras 65, 66). Kelvin observed that, in certain circumstances, the two sets of laws are formally the same; so that concepts used in the one field have formal analogues in the other. Maxwell argued, however, that these formally analogous concepts do not have the same *ontological* status. In particular, he claimed that the electrical potential at a point in a field, which is the formal analogue of the temperature at a point in a conductor, is not, as temperature is, a genuine physical magnitude. Physically, he said, *potential difference* has effects, but not *potential*, whereas temperature has effects as well as, and independently of, temperature differences.

Whether Maxwell was right about this particular case does not matter. What is important is Maxwell's insight that causal connectivity is what characterizes real things. That is, real things should have a range of different properties, and so be capable of participating in various causal processes. Therefore, we should not expect the properties of a real thing to be given wholly by definition, or to be just those it is postulated as having in some particular theory. Rather, we should expect it to have properties, and hence effects, other than these, and so to manifest itself in different ways. Consider place, time and direction, for example. If mere position in space and time has no effects, and space is isotropic, then place, time and direction are all "mere scientific concepts" by Maxwell's criterion. The physically real quantities here (assuming a Newtonian world) are just distance, time-interval and angle; for these are the properties that make a difference in physical causal processes.

While the main argument for scientific realism is thus limited in its applicability to certain of the entities postulated in our causal process theories, it is important to appreciate the full strength of the argument. It is not, as I see it, just an argument for the existence of material particles, and things that are constituted of them. It is also, *prima facie*, an argument for the existence of certain properties, for example the properties that these particles are supposed to have. For, we may ask: why do the fundamental particles behave *as if* they had these properties? The only satisfactory answer seems to be: because they *actually do* have these properties. To try to reduce them (the properties) to sets of material particles, as Smart was (and I believe is still) inclined to do, is to make a mystery of the similarity of behaviour of these particles. For this fact could hardly be explained by their common set membership, if it is being denied that there is anything that unites the members of this set, save that they have the same general name. The set-theoretic reduction of particle properties to sets of particles thus seems contrary to the spirit of scientific realism. Indeed, such a reduction is more in keeping with logical atomism than scientific realism, because it seeks to cut our ontology to fit our logic, rather than our science.

The main argument for scientific realism is also, apparently, an argument for the existence of forces, fields, spatiotemporal relationships and many other kinds of things. If we are not to embrace *global* scientific realism, we must at least show how its application is limited to what we may reasonably believe in. Unfortunately, this is not an easy task, because the main argument for scientific realism is not a sufficient guide. The difficulty lies in deciding when the world behaves *as if* entities of such-and-such a kind existed, and when postulation of entities of this kind is necessary to explain this fact. Consider the question of whether forces exist. It seems clear enough that the world behaves as if forces both existed and acted more or less as they are supposed to act. But it is doubtful whether we must suppose them to exist to explain this fact. Or again, what about points in space–time? Here there seems to be a clash of intuitions about whether the world behaves as if they existed. Certainly, they are postulated to exist in most physical geometries, but they are not considered to be causes. So my inclination is to say that the main argument does not apply to them.

The aim of the remaining sections of this chapter is to sketch the kind of ontology I think the main argument for scientific realism implies, given the current state of scientific knowledge.

The ontology

Ontological reduction

We say that things of a kind A can be reduced ontologically to elements of the kinds B if and only if it can be shown (a) that As would not exist unless elements of the kinds B existed; and (b) that As consist of elements of just these kinds. That is, the existence of elements of the kinds B must be severally necessary and jointly sufficient for the existence of As. If As can be so reduced, then we may say that the existence of As *depends on* the existence of elements of the kinds B. If elements of these kinds cannot themselves be ontologically reduced, then we may say that they *exist fundamentally*. But the aim of ontology is to say what kinds of elements must be supposed to exist fundamentally. In other words, its aim is to say what kinds of things we really need for an ontological reduction of everything there is.

I do not require that things that exist fundamentally should also be capable of existing independently of each other. For it is possible, given these definitions, that the elements to which a thing may be reduced should turn out to be ontologically *interdependent*. Thus, it is consistent to hold that the universe consists of fundamental parti-cles, and their basic properties, although neither could exist without the other. Some philosophers will take a different view on this, and insist that things in the basic categories should be capable of exist-ing independently of things in other categories. However, I can see no good reason to insist on this independence assumption, at least across categories. A good deal of ontological reduction is possible without it, and, as we shall see, it would prevent the construction of some very neat and satisfying ontologies to demand it.

For reasons to be given shortly, we should expect an ontology to be highly reductive in each of the basic categories of existents it assumes. I stress, however, that the economy required concerns kinds of things rather than their individual instances. This is because the reductiveness of an ontology is unaffected by how many individ-ual things we may have to suppose there are of any given kind. David Lewis has argued this in his defence of modal realism (1973: 87). I endorse the point, without endorsing the theory he was defending.

The basic items in any given category must be simple, that is, not constituted of, or divisible into, other things in this category. For if they were not simple, they would be reducible to these other things, and so would not exist fundamentally. Thus, if quarks are postulated as basic items in a category of physical entities, then it must be sup-posed that they are not reducible to any more fundamental things in this category. Nor can it be that the basic items of a given category are reducible to things in other categories. If, for example, we have an ontology that includes fundamental particles as basic items, we cannot consider the particles to be just co-instantiations of particle properties at points in space. For this would be to make points in space and particle properties the more fundamental categories.

Comprehensiveness, reductiveness and explanatory power

An ontology seeks to establish a system of categories of the sorts of things that exist fundamentally, and to explain how other things either fit into these categories, or depend ontologically on the things that do. To be acceptable, it should be a good theory by the usual criteria for theory evaluation. However, because an ontology must be a supremely general theory to be any good, comprehensiveness must be a very important consideration in evaluating an ontology. Other kinds of theories can afford to be more restricted in scope. On the other hand, we should not expect an ontology to be predictive, as we would a scientific theory, because such a general theory as an ontology must be is bound to be programmatic. It would be an extraordinary ontology if it were able to predict the existence of some new kind of entity, although I do not say that this is impossible. However, a good ontology should be able to influence our beliefs about what there is in the sort of way that a good moral theory should be able to influence our beliefs about what is right. That is, by systematizing, and seeking to explain and justify our beliefs, it should ultimately correct them.

An ontology should also be highly reductive, not only because we want it to be as simple as possible, but also because differences between supposedly fundamental existents must be held to be inexplicable. For example, when there were just a few fundamental particles known to exist, they could all be accepted as basic items in an ontology. But when the number grew to 100 or more, we should have had to suppose that all this diversity could exist without any underlying structure that would explain it, if we still wished to accept all of these particles as ultimate constituents of matter. Some diversity, somewhere in the fundamental categories, may be needed to explain the diversity that we know exists. But too much diversity would leave too many differences at the fundamental level unexplained; and to accept the ontology would then be to suppose that these differences are finally inexplicable. Consequently, it is a considerable virtue of an ontology if the number of basic items posited for each category is small.

As with any theory, the most important virtue of an ontology is its explanatory power. There is not much point in eliminating a category of things from an ontology, if it does not increase our understanding to do so. The Humean reduction of causes to regularities, for example, made possible an ontology without a category of causal relationships. But it did so at the expense of our understanding of reality. David Hume's own psychological account of the genesis of our causal concepts is certainly unsatisfactory, and epistemological theories about the nature of causal laws do not explain their apparent necessity to everyone's satisfaction. An ontology that included a category of causes, and explained more, might be better than one that was more highly reductive, but explained less. Reductiveness is not an autonomous virtue, but is derivative from considerations of simplicity and the concern of ontologists not to leave too much diversity unexplained at the fundamental level.

According to the mechanistic ontology, which was commonly accepted after Newton as sufficient for the material world, all physical changes are fundamentally changes of position. Even for Descartes, the world consisted just of matter in motion. Consequently, the regularity theory of causation would allow all causal relationships to be understood as being fundamentally spatiotemporal. This mechanistic ontology had the advantage of being highly reductive. However, since the advent of quantum theory, mechanism is no longer tenable, and the prospect of reducing all changes to changes of position no longer exists. Therefore, other kinds of changes must be envisaged as being at least as primitive. In particular, the sorts of interactions that occur between fundamental particles, which cannot be analysed simply as changes of position, may be in a category of their own, and not reducible to anything else. If so, then perhaps we can reduce all causal processes to these primitive causal interactions between the fundamental particles. I shall consider this possibility in the section "The ontology of causation" below.

The ontological reduction of physical entities

In the category of physical entities I would include everything that is thought to possess energy. The category includes all material objects, all of the fundamental particles and the Schrödinger waves of quantum mechanics that transmit energy in all physical causal processes.

It does not include numbers, sets, propositions, sentences or other abstract particulars. It does not include properties or relationships. And it does not include forces. If we believe that any things of these kinds exist, and are not reducible to things in the category of physical entities, then we must say to what other category or categories they belong.

In the heyday of positivism, when laws were thought of as just correlations between observables, some philosophers of science argued against the existence of fields. For example, P. W. Bridgman did so in his book *The Logic of Modern Physics* ([1927] 1954: 59). Bridgman sought to eliminate fields by construing statements about them as being strictly about the dispositions that are established in charged particles, or whatever the fields are supposed to act on. His view was that particles that are accelerated by fields are actually accelerated by the systems that we say generate the fields. But these fields are really fiction. The systems act directly on the particles and create the dispositions they undoubtedly possess.

There are, however, good reasons to be realists about fields. One such reason derives from the main argument for scientific realism. The best theory we have of the causal interactions that take place between particles is that of wave mechanics. And this theory is unquestionably one of the most successful theories in the whole history of physics. Therefore, by the normal criteria employed by scientific realists, one ought to be a wave mechanical realist. This is a causal explanatory theory, and the Schrödinger waves that are required as mediators in interactions between particles are essential to the explanations provided by this theory. For they are the carriers of the energy that is transferred in these interactions, and without them energy would not be conserved. Therefore, by the main argument for scientific realism, we should be realists about fields.

Next, an ontology of fundamental particles, interacting without the mediation of fields, is untenable, given that some of the fundamental laws of quantum mechanics are expressed as wave equations, and that the energy transfer processes involved in particle interactions are best described by these equations. Indeed, an ontology of fields, in which particles are understood to be more or less stable wave packets, is now generally accepted. Moreover, the distinction between particles and resonances is hard to make,[4] and particles are coming to be seen as field phenomena, which cannot exist except in the fields in which they are embedded. Therefore, the direction of ontological reduction that now seems most plausible is from particles to fields.

Even classically, there is good reason to believe in fields, since they have always been required as the bearers of potential energy. When opposite charges are separated, it is conventional to say that they each acquire a certain amount of potential energy. But in a classical ontology of particles, moving under the influence of mutually attractive or repulsive forces, potential energy can be understood only dispositionally, if fields are not considered to be real. For the particles are not *changed* in any way as a result of being separated. Therefore, if we do not have fields in our ontology, we must say that, in acquiring potential energy, the particles simply gain a disposition to accelerate towards each other. To explain a disposition, however, we need a categorical basis for it.[5] A field that is created in the process of separating the particles, and which bears the potential energy, is the best explanation we have.

If fields are the more basic kinds of physical entities, this raises important questions about their nature. What sorts of things are they? The evidence seems to be that they are entities that are propagated as waves, but act as particles; the probability of a field acting at a point being a function of the wave amplitude at that point. The difficult question is how this is possible. If the energy is localized somewhere in the field, then there is a problem of explaining the interference phenomena that are observed (for instance in the "two-slit" experiment). If the energy is dispersed throughout the field in the process of propagation, then there is the problem of explaining

---

4. See Eyvind H. Wichmann, *Berkeley Physics Course 4* (New York: McGraw-Hill, 1971) for an excellent discussion on this point.

5. In this passage, I seem to be endorsing David Armstrong's theory of dispositional properties. However, this is not what I was doing. I was simply pointing out that a dispositional property needs a substantial location, which is different. And the only plausible location of the potential energy, it seemed to me, is in the space that separates the particles. So, this space must contain something that is substantial.

how the field can collapse, apparently instantaneously, in the process of particle interaction. For this would seem to imply that energy localization may occur instantaneously, or at least at superluminal velocities. I favour the second view, despite its apparent conflict with relativity theory, because a probability field seems more like a mathematical fiction than a physical entity. What is physical has energy, and if fields are physical entities, then the energy must be dispersed throughout them. In any case, the empirical evidence is that there is an upper limit to the speed of energy transmission, not that there is an upper limit to the speed of energy localization. These two kinds of processes must be just fundamentally different.

The ontological reduction of events

Scientific realists must suppose that all events are physical events, where these events are changes in physical systems. Such events always involve changes in the form or distribution of energy. So, without loss of generality, we may define a physical event as any change of distribution of energy in any of its forms. Of course, many events, so understood, will be phenomenologically indistinct parts of larger events, and so not thought of as separate events. Nevertheless, this definition of "physical event" fits well with our conception of a physical entity and it does not include any changes that are clearly not physical. It does not include mental events, for example, if these are not changes in the distribution of energy in the universe.

Not all physical events have the same ontological status. Changes of shape, for example, are ontologically reducible to systematic changes in the relative positions of parts of things; and changes that occur in them are ontologically reducible to changes in their parts, and so on. But not "and so on" indefinitely. For we now know that there are many physical changes that are not reducible to changes of position. The question for ontology, then, is what sorts of physical events must we consider to be those that occur most fundamentally.

Changes of position within physical systems are certainly physical events by the definition we have given; and there is no reason to suppose that they are reducible to any more fundamental physical changes. All attempts to develop causal theories of space–time, which would permit the reduction of spatiotemporal relationships to causal ones, have so far been unsuccessful, and the prospects for their success in future are not good (see Heathcote 1984). The temporal order is perhaps identical to the causal order, and hence reducible to it, as Hans Reichenbach (1958: para. 21) once argued. But the complete reduction of spatiotemporal relationships to causal ones does not seem to be possible. Therefore, we should, at least provisionally, recognize changes of position occurring within physical systems as a primitive category of events.

In addition to changes of position, I think we also need to recognize that there are some essentially different kinds of changes occurring in the interactions between fundamental particles. On present theory, as I understand it, these interactions can be reduced to four basic kinds – the strong, the weak, the electromagnetic and the gravitational – although there is reason to think that some reduction in the number of kinds of basic interactions may be possible.[6] These basic kinds of interactions are thought to be governed by characteristic conservation and symmetry principles, and the general theory of particle interactions based on these principles is elegant, comprehensive and highly reductive. Therefore, it is reasonable to speculate that all physical events are ultimately reducible to interactions of these kinds, and the characteristic wave–particle emissions they produce.

The ontology of causation

The ontology of events I have now outlined immediately suggests an ontology for causal relationships, for it is plausible to suppose that all causal interactions are reducible to basic interactions between fundamental particles. Thus, if the billiard ball A collides with the billiard ball B, then this event is presumably just the sum of the interactions between their particles; and the subsequent motions of A and B are the continuing consequents of these interactions (compounded by

---

6. This possibility is discussed by Daniel Z. Freedman and Peter van Nieuwenhuizen in "Supergravity and the Unification of the Laws of Physics", *Scientific American* **239** (February 1978), 126–43.

those of any further interactions there may be between the balls and the table or other things in their surroundings).

I postulate that no causes are required to sustain a continuing consequence of causal interaction – such as an inertial motion, or the propagation of an electromagnetic wave. These chains of events will continue indefinitely, or until they become involved in some new basic interactions. The only causes involved in these processes, I wish to say, are the interactions that would initiate, change or destroy such motions or waves. The case for regarding inertial motion as a kind of "natural" motion, not requiring any cause to sustain it, has been argued at length in the literature (see Ellis 1965). The case for taking a similar view of electromagnetic radiation is also compelling, although I have never seen it argued. It is that there is no good reason to distinguish radically between electromagnetic (such as gamma) radiation, on the one hand, and alpha, beta and other forms of radiation resulting from particle interactions, on the other. If the motions of the latter are considered to be inertial, then those of the former should be too. Let us call any motions such as these that require no causes to sustain them "energy transfer processes".

A basic problem for the theory of causation is to say how causes are related to their effects. Plausibly, the answer is that they are related somehow by energy transfer processes. Certainly, many causes act positively to produce their effects by these processes. But, while this answer may be on the right track, it will not do as it stands. For there are some causes that produce their effects, not by transferring energy to the sites of these effects, but by blocking or modifying energy transfers to them which would otherwise have occurred. (For example, I may darken my room by pulling the blinds.) Let us say that causes that act in these ways do so "negatively". The issue is further complicated by the fact that an effect may be produced by a combination of positively and negatively acting causes, which may be acting either in series or in parallel. However, it would seem to be at least a necessary condition for an event A to be causally related to an event B that it be serially related to B by some such combination of processes.

This ontological account of causation is comprehensive, highly reductive and offers a satisfying explanation of the nature and variety of causal relationships. It identifies their direction as that of the energy transfer processes involved; it explains why there is an upper limit to the speed with which causal influences may be transmitted (because there is an upper limit to the speed of energy transfer); it explains how there can be unique, never to be repeated, cause-and-effect relationships, which regularity theories cannot satisfactorily account for; and it explains how causes may operate in an indeterministic world, which no regularity or natural necessitation theory of causation can do. According to my ontological theory, all causal influences are transmitted by processes that are fundamentally indeterministic.

These energy transfer processes are also said to transmit the forces that are involved in particle interactions. Thus, the electromagnetic force is supposed to be transmitted by photons or electromagnetic waves; the strong force is thought to be transmitted by gluons, gravitation by gravitons, and so on. All of the changes that occur in particle interactions are said to be produced by the actions of these forces. Now, this way of speaking suggests that forces are just kinds of causal influences, and, so conceived, there is good enough reason to believe in them. If there are four basic kinds of causal interactions between particles, there are four basic kinds of causal influences.

There is another way of speaking about forces, however, that suggests that they are necessarily present when the effects they are said to produce occur, and are necessarily productive of these effects. This is the classical conception of force as an entity that intervenes between a physical cause and its effect, but is not itself a physical cause. For reasons I have given elsewhere, I see no reason to believe in forces of this kind. In principle, they are eliminable from physics,[7] and if we have an ontology that includes primitive causal influences, we are not left having to believe in a Humean world. When we know how fields and particles interact, and how the effects of their interactions are transmitted, we know what there is to know about primitive causes, and how they are related to their effects.

---

7. For a proof of this see my "The Existence of Forces", *Studies in the History and Philosophy of Science* 7 (1976), 171–85.

Properties and relationships

The main argument for scientific realism requires us to be realists about physical properties and relationships as well as about forces (conceived as modes of causal influence). For there are infinitely many effects that such forces may have, depending on the physical properties and relationships of their sources and objects. These physical properties and relationships must therefore be part of the causal story of why things behave as they do. Thus, we must say that the world behaves as if things had these physical properties, and were related physically to each other in these ways; and the best explanation of this fact must be that they really do have these properties, and are in fact so related.

It is not easy to say what sorts of things physical properties and relationships are. Consider properties. Some would simply identify them with sets of individuals (every set being a property); others would say that they are universals that may or may not be instantiated in individuals; and some would say that there are no property-universals, only property-instances or tropes that may in fact be similar. However, I am unhappy with all of these accounts of the nature of properties. For reasons to be given presently, I am sure that properties are not just sets of individuals; and the other two theories cannot easily account for the structure we find in the system of the most fundamental properties we know about. How, for example, does one explain the relationship between different properties of the same kind, like spin ½ and spin ¾, on a theory of universals or tropes? What seems to be needed for science is an ontology that recognizes the fundamentally quantitative nature of the most basic properties of particles and fields; and such an ontology must somehow include such multi-valued properties or their values as primitive.

I do not know how to construct such an ontology, because I have no adequate theory of what quantities or, more generally, what multi-valued properties are. They are not universals as they are usually understood, because universals are not multi-valued. Universals may be multiply instantiated; but different instances of a property-universal must be the same in respect of this property, that is, they must be single-valued. In *Basic Concepts of Measurement* (1966: ch. 2), I argued that quantities are the objective linear orders into which things possessing them may be arranged, and that the measurement of quantities consists in assigning "numerals" to things according to their positions in these linear orders. By doing so, I sought to avoid the extremes of operationism, which would pointlessly have divided our quantitative concepts according to how they were measured, and a naive realism, which would have located quantities and their magnitudes wholly in the objects possessing them – independently of the existence of anything else. However, I no longer find any of these accounts completely satisfying.

It is easier to say what physical properties and relationships are not than what they are. In formal logic, it is usual to represent a property as a set of individuals, and an n-place relationship as a set or ordered n-tuples of things – thus leaving the question of what sort of thing a property or relationship is wide open. This is fine for the purposes of logic, but it would be a mistake to make too much of the usefulness of this particular representation, and suppose that properties are nothing more than the sets of individuals that possess them, or that relationships are nothing more than the sets of ordered n-tuples that instantiate them. For what has to be explained is what the various members of these sets have in common, and it is not at all helpful to say that they all satisfy the same predicates, for this leaves the point of having these predicates in our language unexplained, and also why, in so many cases, there should be so many cases of predicates in other languages with exactly the same extensions.

Moreover, to regard properties just as sets of individuals, and n-place relationships as sets of ordered n-tuples of individuals, is to make nonsense of the whole idea of discovering a new property or relationship. Sets are defined or constructed, not discovered; and there is nothing easier than defining a new set. Yet scientists surely do discover new properties and relationships, and what they do is by no means trivial. Murray Gell-Mann, for example, was awarded the Nobel Prize for Physics for his discovery of the set of relationships among certain properties of the fundamental particles known as the "Eightfold Way". A consistent scientific realist must hold that this symmetry existed before it was described.

Whatever general account of properties we may eventually give, we may define a physical property as one whose value is relevant, in some circumstances, to how a physical system is likely to act. Thus, it is a property that makes a physical difference. The most fundamental physical properties we know about are the multi-valued properties of fields and fundamental particles. They include such quantities as mass, charge, spin, interaction potential, hypercharge, strangeness, colour, charm, flavour and many others. But perhaps the most important of all multi-valued properties is energy itself. I think a scientific realist must believe that energy exists, and is conserved in all fundamental interactions.

Our account of physical properties should give us the lead for an account of physical relationships. For the most important physical relationships are also quantitative. In many cases, the quantitative relationships we speak about are ontologically dependent on the physical properties of the things related. This is normally the case, for example, when we speak of two things being equal or unequal in respect of some quantity. Therefore, we may not need to have an independent theory of quantitative relationships, if we have an ontology that includes quantitative universals. However, there appears to be at least one class of quantitative relationships that cannot be so reduced, namely, the spatiotemporal ones. For position in space–time does not appear to be a physical property in the sense in which I am here using this term. The laws of nature are supposed to be invariant with respect to position in space–time; therefore, mere position in space–time cannot make a difference to the propensity of a physical system to act in any way. Therefore, we must recognize that there is at least one ontologically irreducible class of physical relationships, namely the spatiotemporal ones.

The theory of multi-valued universals I have proposed as a possible solution to the problem of ontologically reducing the category of properties and relationships to its most basic elements is so far not much more than a suggestion. But if it can be made to work, it promises to yield a theory no less reductive or comprehensive in its own sphere than the reduction of all physical entities to particles and fields.

This ontology is probably not yet complete. For, in addition to the various categories of things that I have described, we probably also need a category of numerical relationships – since there is no reason to suppose that these relationships can be reduced to any of the other categories. And no doubt there are other kinds of things that have not yet been accounted for. However, realism about numerical relationships does not require realism about numbers. For numbers, abstractly considered, belong to the theory of possible numerical relationships, and so are not supposed to be causally effective. They are like geometrical points in this respect. Therefore, a scientific realist is not required to believe in them.

There is also no good reason for a scientific realist to be realistic about sets. For sets are idealized heaps or collections. They have determinate membership; heaps do not. The membership of a set may not vary; but a thing may at one time be, and at another time not be, something that belongs to a given heap. The things that belong to a given collection must belong to the same ontological category; sets are not so restricted. But sets are not supposed to have any causal roles. Like numbers, they are incapable of changing or being changed. Therefore, a scientific realist is not required to believe in them. It may be useful to postulate them for certain purposes, just as it is useful to speak of other sorts of idealized systems. However, a sophisticated scientific realist should not be realistic about every sort of thing it is useful to postulate, but only those things they have to believe in to accept the causal process theories they do.

Smart would probably disagree with me about whether a scientific realist should believe in sets, since I know he was once inclined to believe in an ontology that included them. For example, he was inclined to believe that there is a set of all the negatively charged fundamental particles, as well as these fundamental particles themselves. However, his own argument for scientific realism does not require him to believe in the reality of sets. The world does not behave as if there were such sets, because the sets must exist if and only if all their members exist, and they are, therefore, ontologically reducible to them. But it does behave as if there were certain properties, like that of being negatively charged. And this is reason enough to believe in such properties, as well as in the things that possess them.

The ontology to which a scientific realist is committed does not, therefore, include all of the categories of things Smart would wish to include, and it does include some things of kinds that Smart may not wish to have in his ontology. Nevertheless, Smart's original argument for scientific realism is a powerful one, although it cannot be deployed indiscriminately. We need to understand its scope and limitations to apply it correctly. When we do, we can use it to develop a comprehensive and highly reductive ontology for science. It has been my aim in this chapter to show how this can be done.

Postscript

In 1987, when I wrote this paper, it may seem that I was then living a kind of double life. For it is manifestly an essay in metaphysical realism. Yet, at the time of writing it, I was vigorously defending internal realism (see Ellis 1988a,b, 1990). So, this essay appears to be totally out of phase with my other work at this time. But this is more appearance than reality. For my evaluative theory of truth allowed me to say anything that I thought I was rationally justified in saying. And what I said in this essay is precisely what I thought I was rationally justified in saying about the nature of reality. What is unusual about it is that I did not reach these conclusions by considering which of the laws or theories of science that I considered to be true. I reached them by asking what the world must be supposed to be like, given the causal process theories that most of us accept.

My realist friends mostly took the view that I was being disingenuous: I simply could not marry a theory that is realistic about atoms, electromagnetic fields, causal powers and processes, and spatiotemporal and numerical relations with an evaluative theory of truth. But I could not see why not. In all sincerity, I used to ask: which of the claims I make about the nature of reality are the ones that you think I am not epistemically justified in believing? I think that most of my critics thought that I was not epistemically justified in believing any of them. But any reasons that they were able to give for believing in the reality of these things seemed to me to be ones that I could just as happily accept. And my realist friends used to get very angry with me. They insisted, for example, that to be a realist, I had to accept a correspondence theory of truth. "Oh", I said, "is that what I am epistemically justified in believing? Of course, if I am epistemically justified in believing it, then the correspondence theory of truth must be true in my sense."

But, as I explained in Chapter 1, I was beginning to have doubts about the coherence of my overall position. So, I put this paper aside in order to focus on the main issue. And my book *Truth and Objectivity* (1990) was precisely about this. It was, in fact, an attempt to prove that acceptance of an evaluative theory of truth is compatible with belief in the existence of an objective world of the kind that a realistic interpretation of the causal process theories of science entails. Here is a quote from the Introduction to that book.

> This book traces an argument from a scientific ontology to [a] theory of truth [which preserves the classical properties of truth, and coheres with scientific realism], and outlines an epistemology that will take us back to the ontology. The argument is circular, but none the worse for that, since the aim is to establish coherence. The ontology is the kind of theory of reality one would expect a scientific realist to hold, for it is constructed on the assumption that currently accepted scientific accounts of the nature of reality are the best theories available. It admits no more entities than appear to be necessary for these accounts to be viable. In contrast, the theory of truth I propose to defend is not one that is widely accepted by scientific realists. It is an evaluative theory in the sense that it identifies truth with what it is right to believe, and it is a naturalistic theory in that it is embedded in a naturalistic epistemology. (1990: 2)

Having completed this task, I thought successfully, I thought that I was now at liberty to explore the metaphysics of scientific realism without regard to truth theory. A good metaphysics of reality, I thought, was just a good general theory about the nature of reality; and truth does not come into it. But on reflection now, I think a theory of truth really does come into it. For a good general theory about the nature of reality would have to explain how what we believed on the basis of our best science about the world supervened on what our general theory postulated. That is, it would have to show how, in general terms, our best scientific theories corresponded to reality.

Shortly after completing the manuscript for *Truth and Objectivity*, I began work on the theory of natural kinds. I did so for two reasons. First, I had speculated, back in the 1980s, before setting out to write that book, that the world itself might be a one of a natural kind, and that the laws of nature could, perhaps, be regarded as being of its essence. I wanted to give more thought to this possibility. Secondly, the concluding chapter of *Truth and Objectivity* contained the following intriguing suggestion, which I thought needed to be followed up:

> [O]ntology is not just about what it is right to believe. It is about what fundamental categories of things exist, and what their essential natures are. It is about what natural kinds of things must be supposed to exist to account for everything we believe in. But if we can come up with an ontology of natural kinds which is adequate, and we can say what the essences of the fundamental categories of things are, then the best explanation of the fact that we can do all this is that these natural kinds really do exist, and have the natures we ascribe to them. If the categories simply reflected our interests, or our particular epistemic perspective, then this would be a remarkable and inexplicable fact. (1990: 285)

"The Ontology of Scientific Realism" (1987 and here) is remarkable for its innocence, and for what it presaged. It was not an essay in which I was consciously rejecting the internal realist perspective that I had defended throughout the 1980s. I thought it was entirely consistent with my views on truth that I should try to develop the best general theory of the nature of reality that I could. For that is what the evaluative theory of truth requires that I should try to do. The result was the outline of an ontological theory that I still find almost entirely acceptable. I am still realistic about properties of the kinds postulated as effective in the causal mechanisms of scientific theories. I believe in the existence of irreducible spatiotemporal and numerical relationships. I am still a realist about causal powers, and about events and processes of the kinds postulated in our best scientific theories. I am also a realist about fields of the kinds involved in energy transmission processes, and I still believe in the existence of two fundamentally different kinds of processes in nature: those involved in the transmission of energy, and those that appear to be nothing more than instantaneous changes of state. Finally, I have now taken up the suggestion, again without conscious awareness that this is what I was doing, that there is need for a category of quantitative universals in ontology. My new entities are what I call "dimensions" (see Chapter 5). They are more general than the kinds of entities I proposed back in 1987. They include what I then called "quantitative universals", but they also include some other respects in which things may be either the same or different.

What I have in fact done since the publication of *Truth and Objectivity* is largely try to develop the ontology of scientific realism on which this book is based. "With a little help from my friends", as the Beatles used to say, I have written extensively on the theory of dispositonal properties, which include all of the basic properties in nature that are not categorical. I have developed the theory of natural kinds into a sophisticated theory of the nature of reality. I have argued that the world itself is a member of natural kind, even if it is, in fact, the only one of its kind. I have developed a theory of laws of nature, which explains not only their natural necessity, but also their hierarchical structure. My aim in this book is to continue the process of working out the metaphysical theory outlined in "The Ontology of Scientific Realism", to extend it to include a form of quantum mechanical realism, which depends on there being at least two radically distinct natural kinds of processes in nature, and to apply the theory with a view to reforming other areas of study in which assumptions are evidently made about the nature of reality.

3

ESSENTIALIST REALISM

In *Scientific Essentialism* (2001), I attempted to develop an ontology of the kind envisaged in my 1987 essay.[1] First, I argued that the ontology required for a scientific worldview should be a highly structured one. For one of the most striking facts about the world is the apparent dominance of natural kinds. There appears to be an immense hierarchy of substantive natural kinds, that is, natural kinds whose instances are what Aristotle would have called "substances". For every different chemical substance (and there are hundreds of thousands of them) would appear to be a member of a natural kind. Each kind of chemical substance would seem (a) to be categorically distinct from all of the others, and (b) to have its own essential properties and structures. Moreover, the chemical kinds would all seem to belong in a natural hierarchy, the more general ones having essences that are included in those of the more specific. Given that this hierarchy of natural kinds exists, this is plausibly a significant fact about the world that should be reflected in any satisfactory ontology of scientific realism. The world is evidently not just a physical world, as I had assumed in the 1970s, but a highly structured one.

Secondly, there appears to be a vast hierarchy of dynamic natural kinds, that is, natural kinds whose instances are events or processes.

---

1. Chapter 2, above.

Indeed, everything that happens in the world seems to consist of events or processes that are instances of such kinds. Every chemical change, for example, is one of a kind that can be represented uniquely by a particular chemical equation, and no other kind of chemical change can be represented by this same equation. It is plausible, therefore, to suppose that there is a natural hierarchy of dynamic natural kinds as well as one of substantive kinds. And, if this is true, then this may also be a significant fact about the structure of reality that should be reflected in the ontology of scientific realism. Yet philosophers have rarely spoken about natural kinds, except in relation to biological species, which is unfortunate, because biological species are not natural kinds in the same strict sense. If they are taken in historical perspective, biological species can be seen to merge into one another, without any sharp or natural divisions between them. Biological species are certainly like natural kinds in many ways, but do not have all of the same properties. I call them "cluster kinds", as I shall later explain.

Natural kinds, as I understand them, are species of universals. Classically, universals are conceived as being natural properties or relations, that is, properties or relations that exist in nature independently of our knowledge and understanding. Substantive and dynamic natural kinds are not properties or relations, but formally they are like them. From the point of view of a physicalist, the most general substantive kind must be the class of all physical systems, which is a global kind that would include all other substantive kinds as species. And, the most general dynamic kind must be the class of all self-contained physical events or processes, which is also a global kind. It is one that includes all other dynamic kinds as species. At the other extreme, we have the most specific of all species within any given category: the infimic ones. These are species that have no subspecies. The kind "electron", for example, would appear to be an infimic species of the substantive kind "fundamental particle". Electron–positron annihilation would appear to be an infimic species of the dynamic kind "annihilation process".[2]

---

2. As in classical universals theory, it is important to distinguish infimic species from instances. If the property of having mass is a generic universal, that of having a mass of one gram is an infimic species of mass. But this infimic species of mass is itself a universal that may have many instances. It may, for

If I am right that there is a natural kinds structure of the universe, then this has important implications for metaphysics. For the existence of a natural kinds structure is not an empirical discovery. It is not anything that you will find in your physics or chemistry textbooks. It is just a metaphysical hypothesis concerning the structure of reality that is being proposed in order to explain some of the many precise, and apparently exact, regularities that are to be found in nature. These same regularities could be due to chance. Or they could be attributed to the existence of universal laws of nature, which dictate, from the outside, as it were, how things that are structured in certain ways must behave, or how changes of state or motion must occur. But, if we are not theists, and do not accept the divine command theory of the laws of nature, which was presupposed by those who invented the term, it is hard to understand why there should be any such laws of nature, or how they could influence the things they are supposed to influence. However, if things are bound to behave according to their natures, or to display the intrinsic causal powers they possess according to the natures of these powers, then we can go some way towards explaining why things are bound to behave as they do without having to suppose that there are laws of nature to which they are necessarily obedient.

As Smart said many years ago, belief in scientific realism requires the rejection of cosmic coincidences. If you believe in their possibility, he said, you might just as well believe in "scientific phenomenalism", which was his term for the empiricist reduction of science to meter readings, and other observational data. His point was that every uniformity that you could ever observe could, in principle, always be explained as a cosmic coincidence. But the hypothesis of a natural kinds structure of the world, within which things are intrinsically disposed to behave[3] according to their essential natures,

---

example, be instanced in this lump of iron, or in that one. Such property-instances are said to be tropes of the property in question. Likewise, we may refer to particular electrons as tropes of the kind "electron", or to particular examples of electron–positron annihilations as tropes of the kind "electron–positron annihilations".

3. For the concept of intrinsicality that is being used here, see my *Scientific Essentialism*, 26–32.

in ways depending on the circumstances in which they happen to find themselves, dispenses with the need for cosmic coincidences, and also makes it unnecessary to fall back on theism to explain the known uniformities in nature. It implies, for example, that things must, of metaphysical necessity, behave as their natures dictate. The hypothesis of a natural kinds structure of the world thus provides a satisfactory framework for an ontologically plausible theory of the truthmakers for most of the laws of nature.[4]

It not only provides an ontologically plausible theory of the truthmakers of particular laws: it also explains their hierarchical structure. In general, the laws of nature must be supposed to be just true descriptions of the ways in which things are intrinsically disposed to behave: of how they would behave if they existed as closed and isolated systems. Thus, the most general laws will describe how physical systems generally are intrinsically disposed to behave; and the more specific ones will describe how more specific kinds of physical systems must be disposed. The hypothesis also explains the peculiar kind of necessity that we normally attribute to laws of nature. For the intrinsic properties of the natural kinds are plausibly just their real essences. And, if this is so, then it is metaphysically necessary that things of these kinds will always behave as these properties dictate, unless they are somehow gazumped, swamped or interfered with. The Lagrangian law of least action, for example, is necessarily one that applies to all closed and isolated systems. For, plausibly, all physical systems are essentially Lagrangian.

In *Scientific Essentialism*, I argued that we need a structured ontology such as this one, because ontologies have much work to do. They must be capable of deciding whether a proposed truthmaker for anything that we may think we know is ontologically plausible, or which of two process theories is ontologically to be preferred, if alternative theories of this kind happen to be available. Structured ontologies are certainly capable of doing a great deal of such useful work, as Helmholtz demonstrated with his own structured metaphysical theory. So, we should judge ontologies not just on the basis

---

4. I am not sure that all laws of nature are made true in this way. The second law of thermodynamics, for example, would appear to be an exception.

of their economy, as many philosophers seem inclined to do, but also on their capacity to synthesize the knowledge we have, and thus accommodate or exclude any new knowledge that we may acquire. Hume's ontology of metaphysically independent events is certainly an economical one. But it does not readily accommodate what we think we know. For example, it makes a great mystery of causation, and even of continuing existence. If all events are loose and separate, as Hume argued, then the successive states of objects must also be loose and separate. And, if this is so, then we can have no good reason to believe that anything that now exists will continue to exist. This would not matter much if there were plausible solutions to such problems that added no more structure to reality than Hume himself proposed. But no such solutions are known.

The properties that have significant roles in the causal process theories of the sciences are mostly causal powers, that is, properties whose identities depend on what they dispose their bearers to do. Indeed, the most fundamental properties of objects would all appear to be like this, as Helmholtz believed. Even mass is arguably just another causal power. For massive bodies all necessarily have the quantitative property "mass" to some degree. And we cannot explain the masses of bodies as being simply derived from the masses of their constituents. For the energy that is required to hold the constituents together also affects the mass of a substance. But even if such an answer were available, we should only have explained the masses of bodies by reference to the masses of their parts. How then should we account for the masses of the most fundamental constituents? A causal power, such as mass, can be dependent on the causal powers of its constituents. But a causal power can never be dependent on anything that does not have any causal powers. And, if matter has an ultimate atomic structure, then we must eventually get down to things that have causal powers that do not depend on the causal powers of their parts. Perhaps causal power dependencies go all the way down: to the parts of the parts of the parts, and so on. Or should we say, as Hume would have said, that the causal powers of things are illusions due to regularities? I think not. For to say this, is to embrace cosmic coincidences of precisely the kind that Smart railed against. The best answer is that causal powers such as mass are not illusions, and that, if the question "Why do things have mass?" can eventually be answered, it will be because the causal powers of massive bodies can be shown to be dependent on other causal powers. Therefore, at the most fundamental level, there must be some irreducible causal powers.

Accepting this conclusion, Caroline Lierse and I (Ellis & Lierse 1994) wrote a paper on dispositional properties, that is, properties, such as causal powers, that dispose their bearers to behave in certain ways, or ranges of ways. We approached the subject believing that there are, in reality, two kinds of properties, dispositional and categorical. But we did not accept any of the theories of dispositional properties that were then currently on offer. Specifically, we argued against David Armstrong's strong categoricalism, that is, the thesis that all basic properties are categorical, and also against Sydney Shoemaker's strong dispositionalism, according to which all genuine properties are dispositional. Our position was dispositionalist about causal powers, but categoricalist about spatiotemporal and numerical relations. We argued against the three theses concerning dispositions that had been proposed and defended by Elizabeth Prior, Robert Pargetter and Frank Jackson, and we defended the following more radical theses: (a) that there are real irreducible dispositional properties in nature; (b) that causal powers necessarily dispose their bearers to produce effects of certain kinds in certain kinds of circumstances; (c) that such properties are among the essential properties of the natural kinds, and are not necessarily grounded in other properties; and (d) that if P is a causal power that is an essential property of things of the natural kind K, and L is the law of action of P, to the effect that things that possess P are necessarily disposed to have the effect E in the circumstances of the kind C, then it is metaphysically necessary that things of the kind K will act as L requires. We called our position "dispositional essentialism".

Scientific essentialism[5]

In my most recent books (Ellis 2001, 2002) I elaborated and defended an essentialist ontology, which builds on Ellis & Lierse (1994). The

---

5. This section of the chapter was originally my contribution to a symposium

metaphysical theory I developed was essentialist, in the traditional sense of being about the sources of power and order in the world. It involved the claim that the power and order derive from the world's ultimate constituents, and the structures of which they are capable. That is, the new essentialism was one that assumed that the dynamism and structure of nature are immanent in the world, rather than imposed on it, as if by God. To explain the evident structure and dynamism of the world, it was argued that the ultimate constituents of reality must either be or have distinctive causal powers, be capable of participating in distinctive ways in various structures, and belong to natural kinds that are distinguished from each other by their real essences. It was accordingly argued that the world has a fundamental natural kinds structure, and that what happens in the world depends on the essential properties of the things of these kinds, and the kinds of structures that can exist.

In this section, I shall: (a) describe my original theory of natural kinds; (b) outline an essentialist ontology based on this theory; and (c) derive an essentialist theory of laws of nature that adequately explains their natural necessity and hierarchical structure. In the following section, I shall discuss some of the issues that have been raised concerning the adequacy of this ontology, including a preliminary discussion of the vexing issue of categorical properties. I shall also develop a process theory of substances to replace my earlier one, according to which substances belong to an ontologically independent category.

Natural kinds

Natural kinds exist if and only if there are objective mind-independent kinds of things in nature. Hence, to believe in natural kinds one must believe that things are divided naturally into categorically distinct classes. Supposedly, such naturally distinct classes of things exist only if the members of each natural class have certain intrinsic properties

---

in 2006 at Oriel College, Oxford on *Essentialism: Ancient and Modern*. It is reproduced here with very few changes, except that I have added a section on the causal roles of quiddities.

that distinguish them categorically from the members of all other natural classes of things. A distinctive set of intrinsic properties for a given kind is called its "real essence".

The real essences of natural kinds are to be distinguished from their nominal essences. The real essence of a kind is the set of powers or structures that a thing must have for it to be a thing of that kind. The nominal essence of a kind (whether natural or not) is the set of powers or structures that a thing must have, or perhaps just the set of predicates that must be satisfied by something, for it to be called a thing of that kind. In either case, the statement attributing the essence to the kind is necessarily true. For there is no possible world in which it would be false. But the two kinds of necessity are nevertheless different. The kind of necessity that is associated with real essences is metaphysical or *de re*, while that associated with nominal essences is analytic or *de dicto*. The difference lies not in the strength of the necessity that is attributed to the relationship, but in its grounding. *De re* necessities are grounded in the real world, and have to be discovered by scientific investigation. Specifically, we have to discover what sets of intrinsic properties or structures are required to constitute things of these kinds. *De dicto* necessities are grounded in our linguistic conventions, and can be discovered by competent speakers of the language just by reflecting on how the terms designating the kinds are used. *De re* necessities are thus *a posteriori* and need to be established empirically, whereas *de dicto* necessities are knowable *a priori*.

Natural kinds may be supposed to exist in many different fields of enquiry. Accordingly, we may distinguish between essentialists by their commitments to natural kinds. To be an essentialist in biology, for example, is to believe that there are natural biological kinds, each of which has its own distinctive real essence. To be an essentialist in chemistry is to believe that there are natural chemical kinds having real essences. To be an essentialist in ontology is to believe that at least some of the most fundamental existents in nature are members of natural kinds, and that things of these kinds are distinguished by their own real essences. Aristotle was a biological essentialist. He believed that animal species were natural kinds that were distinguished from one another by their essential natures. Putnam is a chemical essentialist, as his Twin Earth example illustrates. But most of us who would claim to be essentialists without qualification are ontological essentialists. That is, we believe that natural kinds structures go all the way down to the most basic levels of existence. This does not mean that we believe that these same sorts of structures exist at all higher levels. In fact, very few essentialists these days would claim to be economic, or even biological, essentialists. Most would accept chemical essentialism, the case for which appears to be overwhelming, and some form of physical essentialism, but would be sceptical of essentialist claims about the existence of natural kinds at higher levels of complexity.

Every distinct type of chemical substance would appear to be an example of a natural kind, since the known kinds of chemical substances all exist independently of human knowledge and understanding, and the distinctions between them are all real and absolute. Of course, we could not have discovered the differences between the kinds of chemical substances without much scientific investigation. But these differences were not invented by us, or chosen pragmatically to impose order on an otherwise amorphous mass of data. There is no continuous spectrum of chemical variety that we had somehow to categorize. The chemical world is just not like that. On the contrary, it gives every appearance of being a world made up of substances of chemically discrete kinds, each with its own distinctive chemical properties. To suppose otherwise is to make nonsense of the whole history of chemistry since Antoine Lavoisier.

What is true of the chemical kinds is not true of biological species. The existing species of animals and plants are clusters of morphologically similar organisms whose similarities are due to their genetically similar constitutions. Our species concepts are therefore generic cluster concepts. They are not, however, generic kinds that are categorically distinct from one another, as the generic chemical kinds are. The species "elephant" has a number of subspecies, which are subclusters within the elephant cluster. These subspecies are distinct enough to be reliably distinguished morphologically, and sufficiently different genetically to be said to be different kinds of animals. However, if we broadened our vision to include all of the ancestors of the current elephants in the world, we should find, I think, that the morphological clusters, and the genetic clusters that explain them, would shift about as we go back in time, and eventually overlap. Therefore, neither the generic species, nor any subspecies, of elephant is a natural kind in the same sense as the generic and specific chemical kinds are. Chlorine, for example is a generic chemical kind, the species of which include the various isotopes of chlorine. But there is no species of chlorine existing now, or at any other time, that could possibly be a species of any element other than chlorine. Chlorine, the generic kind, has a fixed nature, and each species of chlorine has its own fixed nature.

Not only do natural kinds of substances exist, which are fixed in nature as the chemical kinds are, but there are also natural kinds of processes, which are fixed in nature in the same sort of way. For every chemical equation represents some kind of process of chemical combination or dissolution. Moreover, each such kind of process is categorically distinct from every other kind of process. There are no halfway houses, that is, no processes between which we have arbitrarily to draw a line and say: "This is a chemical process of this kind, represented by this chemical equation, whereas that is a chemical process of this other kind, represented by this other chemical equation". Chemistry presents us with no such choices, as it surely would if the kinds of chemical processes were not categorically distinct. Therefore, if there are substantive natural kinds, as indeed every distinct kind of chemical substance undoubtedly is, then there are also dynamic natural kinds, that is, naturally distinct kinds or events or processes.

To develop the theory of natural kinds, it is important to make a distinction between an infimic species of a kind and an instance of it. An infimic species of a natural kind is any species of the kind that has no subspecies. The class of electrons, for example, is an infimic species of the fundamental particles, because there are no subspecies of electrons. But the class of electrons is itself a natural kind. So it is a species, not an instance. The instances of the fundamental particles are all of the particular fundamental particles that there are in the world. A particular instance of a particle might well be an electron. But if it is, then it is an instance of the species electrons. The class of fundamental particles is a natural kind, but it is not infimic, since it has subspecies. It is, therefore, a generic natural kind.

In the theory presented in *Scientific Essentialism*, there is also a third kind of natural kind, namely, that of natural properties and relations. Natural properties, I argued, are natural kinds of property-instances, that is, tropes or modes, and natural relations are natural kinds of relation-instances. Consider, for example, the property of unit charge, that is, the charge on an electron. This specific charge is an infimic species of the generic property, charge. The specific property, unit charge, is instanced in every electron, and in every other particle in the universe with single negative charge. But, of course, these instances of unit charge are not the electrons themselves, or any of the other particles with single negative charge, since these particles are not tropes of anything other than (perhaps) the corresponding substantive natural kinds. They could not in any case be tropes of unit charge because they are not all identical. An electron and an anti-protron, for example, both have unit negative charge, but no electron is identical to any anti-protron.

Whether this conception of natural properties and relations is accepted or not, every essentialist is committed to what Lewis and Armstrong call "sparse" theories of properties and relations. Sparse theories distinguish sharply between properties and predicates. Predicates are linguistic entities that would not exist if languages did not exist. Properties and relations are universals, or, at least, natural similarity classes. Consequently, the linguistic operations of negation, conjunction and disjunction do not apply automatically to properties, as they do to predicates. Armstrong allows conjunctive universals, but not disjunctive or negative. I do not allow any of these constructed universals automatically, although I concede that there might be universals that are related to other universals as if they were their conjuncts, disjuncts or negations.

The generic natural kinds in every category are ontologically more fundamental than any of their species. For, the generic natural kinds and properties could exist, even though none of their existing species existed. But conversely, no species of a generic kind or property could exist if that generic kind or property did not exist. Therefore, by the usual argument for ontological dependence, the genera must take precedence over their species in the order of being. Armstrong (1997) thinks that the reverse is the case, and that the generic kinds are somehow constituted by their species. His conclusion certainly appeals to our intuitive belief in the ontological primacy of the ultimately specific properties of particulars. Nevertheless, there is a strong argument against this conclusion, quite apart from the one concerning the direction of ontological dependence. It is the argument that the generic kinds cannot be constituted by their species. One might, for example, try to constitute a generic kind as the disjunct of its infimic species. Disjunctive kinds like this are highly suspect in any case, as Armstrong himself has argued. But there is a further, more telling, objection. Probably, there is no object anywhere in the universe with mass $m/2$, where m is the mass of the electron. But the generic kind, mass, surely includes this species of mass as a logical possibility.

The conclusion that generic kinds are ontologically prior to their species has one very important and pleasing consequence: it explains the overriding importance of generic kinds in the order of nature. For the laws of nature would all appear to be concerned with generic kinds (see § "Objects and processes", below.) Quantities are clear cases of generic properties, that is, properties that have specific measures as their infimic species. Therefore, to the extent that the laws of nature are quantitative, they must be concerned with generic kinds.

Essentialist metaphysics

According to the theory developed in *Scientific Essentialism*, the world consists ultimately of things belonging to natural kinds. Three categories of natural kinds were described: substantive, dynamic and tropic. The substantive natural kinds were supposed to include all of the natural kinds of substances. The dynamic natural kinds were postulated to include all of the natural kinds of events and processes, and the tropic natural kinds were supposed to include all of the natural kinds of property and relation tokens (tropes). It was argued that each of these categories of natural kinds is hierarchically structured by the species relation. And, at the summit of each category, I suggested that there ought to be a global kind, which includes and thus unifies all of the other natural kinds in its category. For example, I supposed the global substantive kind to be the class of all physical systems, and the global dynamic kind to be the class of all physical events or processes. At the base of each hierarchy, I argued, there should be a number, possibly an infinite number, of infimic species. That is, there should be various species that have no subspecies. Sometimes these are readily identifiable. Electrons, for example, are presumably infimic species in the category of substances. In the middle grounds of the various hierarchies are all of the generic kinds that lie in between the global kinds and the infimic species. The world was thus assumed to be a highly structured physical world. This was my basic structural hypothesis.

It was also assumed that every natural kind of thing, at every level of generality, has its own distinctive real essence, that is, its own unique set of intrinsic properties or structures in virtue of which things are of the kinds they are. This is the hypothesis of essentialism. For substantive kinds, it was argued that these intrinsic properties or structures must include at least some causal powers, or other dispositional properties. Complex objects may have distinctive structures. Isomers, for example, may be thus distinguished. But as we descend to more elementary things, structures involving relationships between parts necessarily drop out, and, at the most elementary level, there is no structure at all. Therefore, the most elementary things existing in the world must be essentially distinguished from each other not by their structures, but by their dispositional properties alone. Electrons, for example, must be distinguished from other kinds of fundamental particles dispositionally.

The essence of a dispositional property, though, depends on what it does. Hence, the full description of such a property must tell us what things having this property must be disposed to do in the various possible circumstances in which they might exist. If the property is a propensity, then its full description must describe all of its possible effects and the conditional probabilities of their occurring in whatever the given circumstances might be. Therefore, according to the essentialist metaphysic, the most fundamental natural properties must be (a) the dispositional properties of the basic natural kinds, and (b) the properties of the various possible circumstances in which they might exist. To describe the circumstances of a thing's existence, it is necessary to specify what other things exist with which it might interact, what their intrinsic properties and structures are, and how these other things are related spatiotemporally to the thing itself. Essentialist metaphysics therefore seem to require that there be at least two kinds of properties in nature: dispositional properties (causal powers, capacities and propensities) and categorical ones (spatiotemporal and numerical relations).

Laws of nature

Essentialists believe that the laws of nature describe the essences of the natural kinds. This is the thesis of dispositionalism. The global laws describe the essences of the global kinds, and hence refer to all things in their respective categories; the more specific laws refer only to the more specific kinds and their various subspecies. The applications of the laws to specific cases describe the behaviour predicted of the infimic species involved in these cases. If this is true, then there are two important consequences of essentialism for the theory of laws of nature:

(a) There are hierarchies of laws of nature that are uniquely correlated with the hierarchies of natural kinds. Thus:

(i) There are global laws that apply to all things in the global category of substances. Lagrange's principle of least action, for example, is a law that applies to all physical systems. The law of conservation of energy states that every event or process of the global kind, that is, every physical event or process, is intrinsically conservative of energy. I do not know what the global laws are in the category of properties and relations, but some of the most general must surely be the fundamental laws in the theory of quantitative relationships, for example those of spatiotemporal and of numerical relationships.

(ii) There are laws concerning various kinds of substances and fields. The laws of electromagnetism, for example, are very general, but they are not really global. That is, they do not range nonvacuously over all things in any particular category. The laws of chemistry, of particle interactions and of radioactive decay processes are also in the intermediate range. The objects and processes described in these laws are, of course, subject to the global laws, because the global essences are ubiquitous. But the global laws do not entail the more specific ones, which depend on the more specific essences of the kinds to which they refer. What we call the applications of the laws to specific cases are more specific still, since they depend on the essences of the infimic species of the kinds of things involved.

(b) The laws of nature are metaphysically necessary. Thus electrons are necessarily negatively charged. Physical systems are necessarily Lagrangian. Physical processes are necessarily intrinsically conservative of energy. Water is necessarily H_2O. And so on.

If essentialists are right in thinking that the laws of nature describe the essences of the natural kinds, then the laws of nature are in a class of their own. For they are necessary, but neither analytic nor formally logically necessary. Like accidental generalizations, they are *a posteriori*, and can be established only by empirical enquiry, but unlike such generalizations, they are not contingent.

Ontological critique

The metaphysic outlined has been challenged in a number of ways. John Heil (2003, 2005) does not like the theory of universals that is used, and would prefer an ontology of tropes ("modes", in his terminology), grouped by similarity relationships. Stephen Mumford (2005) has questioned the essentialist hypothesis (that every ontologically basic natural kind has its own distinctive real essence). Heil (2005) and Alexander Bird (2005) have supported Shoemaker (1980) in arguing that the fundamental properties in nature must all be causal powers. Joel Katzav (2004) has argued that Lagrange's principle of least action cannot adequately be accounted for on the theory of dispositionalism. Bigelow (1999) has expressed concerns about the theory of counterfactuals to which I am committed, and Armstrong (2002) objects to the Meinongianism of my position. I have replied to all of these objections, but two issues remain of some concern.

First, the ontology I originally proposed to accommodate the new essentialism seems too lavish. It has three interdependent categories of existence (physical objects, physical processes and property instances [tropes]), and three hierarchies of natural kinds (substantive kinds, dynamic kinds and properties). Surely some simplification is possible. Secondly, the category of properties was supposed to include relations. Therefore, numerical and spatiotemporal relations were put in the same category as causal powers. But these would appear to be very different kinds of things, and it is implausible that there should be any overarching theory of things of a global kind that includes these two subcategories. The category of properties and relations thus appears to lack coherence.

Objects and processes

To simplify the ontology, I now wish to argue that physical objects should be regarded as ongoing physical processes.[6] I do so on the ground that they can plausibly be seen as belonging to an important subcategory of processes that includes all of the continuing ones. The continuing processes are to be contrasted with such instantaneous events as photo-emissions, radioactive decays, spin determinations, particle annihilations and other natural displays or interactions. The systems within which such changes of state occur may be spatially extended, but the events of change are not, and cannot be, temporally extended. When, for example, an electron falls from a higher energy level to a lower one, and the system thereby emits a photon, there is thought to be no time taken for this process to occur, and certainly there is no process of accelerating the photon up to speed. The change is, apparently, just an instantaneous change of state. Similarly, when a photon is absorbed at a particular spot on a photographic plate, the distributed energy of the wave packet collapses at this point, and this process of collapse seems to be instantaneous. The same is evidently true of certain quantum-linked events. If, for example, a process generates a pair of entangled electrons, then these two conceptually distinct particles will remain quantum-linked until some interaction, such as a measurement, is made that breaks the linkage. The location, spin or whatever of the first particle is then determined. But the rest of the entangled object is not left unchanged. For the instantaneous change of state that occurs, as a consequence of the measurement, is one that affects the whole entangled system. And, at that point, the wave function for the second of the two particles also undergoes an instantaneous change of state.[7]

---

6. The position I wish to defend is based on the theory of quantum mechanical realism, and is more fully explained in Chapter 4.

7. It may help us to understand Bell's inequality and the phenomena of non-location, if we think of them as being essentially different from those that

Instantaneous processes like these are essentially different from any processes that take time, and the laws concerning them are very different from those concerning other processes. The subatomic processes that do take time are always inertial and continuing, and proceed according to Schrödinger's wave equation. Once they are initiated by an instantaneous change of state they just keep going, unless or until they are brought to an end by another such change of state. The particle might be absorbed, or it might collide with another particle, or it might just decay radioactively. In all of these cases, the inertial motion of the particle is brought to an end by an instantaneous process.

The energy transmission processes, in contrast, are inertial and of limited velocity. They are inertial in the sense that they continue indefinitely unless or until they are terminated by an instantaneous change of state. They are of limited velocity in the way that all signals have limited velocity. The various species of electromagnetic radiation, for example, are all pure energy transmission processes, as are the inertial motions of objects. The limiting velocity for all such processes is that of light. For instantaneous changes of state there is no such limiting velocity. Such changes occur without lapse of time in the rest frames of the systems in which they occur. Until recently, all such events were assumed to be like energy transmission processes, and therefore to be located wholly within the light cones of the events of their initiation. It follows that if causal interactions, decay processes and the like were truly instantaneous, they could have no parts that were separated in space-like ways. This is known as the principle of locality. But nowadays it is recognized that instantaneous changes of state can occur over spatially extended regions, hence violating the principle of locality. However, if the principle of locality is violated, and there is every reason to suppose that it is, then the events or processes in which such

---

involve energy transfers. In Chapter 4 I shall argue that these phenomena are unique to events in an important subcategory of events and processes, namely, that of instantaneous changes of state. Events in this subcategory have very little in common with processes that involve energy transfers. For an up-to-date overview of the issues, see Hilary Putnam, "A Philosopher Looks at Quantum Mechanics (Again)", *British Journal for the Philosophy of Science* **56** (2005), 615–34, and Chapter 4.

violations occur must be essentially different from any processes that are dependent on energy transmissions.

Therefore, at a very fundamental level, the category of natural kinds of processes must be split in two. There are temporally extended continuing processes and spatially extended instantaneous ones. The two subcategories are unified by the principles of conservation of energy, and by certain other conservation principles, but they are split by the mechanism of change. For the mechanism of an instantaneous change of state, if there is one, cannot be anything like that of an energy transmission process. The suggestion that I now wish to make – and this is new – is this: in the process of continuing to exist, all substances belong essentially to the subcategory of continuing processes. For, it is at least plausible to suppose that in continuing to exist all objects display a kind of inertia. In the absence of any external forces, or processes of internal decay (which would change or destroy the objects), their masses, kinetic energies and momenta must all remain the same. The only ways in which they can change are in their relations with other things.

What physical objects all have essentially in common, then, is their inertial continuance. For they are essentially processes of inertially continuing spatial change. A neutron, for example, is an inertial continuant that is a member of a natural kind. It can change its position in relation to other things. But otherwise it will continue to exist exactly as it is, unless or until it is destroyed, either extrinsically in a particle collision, or intrinsically by radioactive decay. Moreover, the intrinsic energy, or mass, of a neutron, must also remain constant while the neutron continues to exist. So, from this point of view too, a neutron's continuing existence must also be considered to be an energy conservation process.

My suggestion, then, is that the category of natural kinds of objects or substances should be regarded simply as a subcategory in the category of the natural kinds of processes, thus reducing the number of basic categories of existents from three to two. The same sorts of hierarchies of natural kinds as those I have postulated before must still exist, but given this analysis of the category of objects, the hierarchy of natural kinds of objects must become just a proper part of the hierarchy of natural kinds of processes. The analysis also implies that we have no further need for substantive universals, other than as a subcategory in the hierarchy of the dynamic universals. This all seems to me to be a considerable reduction in the complexity of my original ontology of natural kinds. Moreover, it is an economy that can be effected without loss of metaphysical explanatory power.

Of course, most physical objects are not purely continuing processes. For most are involved in complex causal interactions with things in their environments. They are interacting because their elementary parts are undergoing instantaneous changes of state owing to collisions with things in their environments, which are also undergoing such changes. Nor is it true that most causal interactions at a macroscopic level are just instantaneous changes of state. For the instantaneous changes of state that occur initially when any two macroscopic objects interact produce energy transmissions, which produce other instantaneous changes of state, which produce other energy transmissions and so on, until the whole process is completed. But these facts do not affect the basic ontology. Fundamentally, there are still just two primitive kinds of events or processes: spatially extended instantaneous ones, and temporally extended local ones.

Properties and relations

In their critiques of my essentialism, Heil (2005) and Bird (2005) both argue that the version of dispositional essentialism defended by Caroline Lierse and I in our 1994 paper (Ellis & Lierse 1994) is too weak. The strong essentialist thesis that they prefer is Shoemaker's (1980) version, according to which all properties are essentially dispositional, not just the recognized causal powers. Shoemaker argued that what makes a property the property it is, that is, what determines its identity, is its potential for contributing to the causal powers of things. But acceptance of this strong version of dispositional essentialism would appear to be incompatible with the view that there are genuine categorical properties in nature, that is, the kind of weak categoricalism that Lierse and I defended in our 1994 paper. Bird's argument was this:

> We do not want our metaphysics of properties to condemn us to necessary ignorance of them. And so we should reject

quidditism.[8] Since categoricalism entails quidditism (strong and weak), we should reject categoricalism too. The problems concerning identity and reference raised by quidditism are immediately resolved by adopting strong dispositional essentialism, the view that the identity of properties is fixed by their essential powers.   (2005: 453)

Heil's case was likewise based on the unknowability of powerless categorical properties. But rather than opt for a world of naked powers, Heil makes the classical Lockean compromise. He thinks that the world is fundamentally one made up of "powerful qualities": a world that is neither one of naked powers nor one that is purely qualitative.

I wish to defend a compatibilist thesis. I want to say that spatial, temporal and numerical relations can have various causal roles without themselves being instances of causal powers. For it normally matters how far things are apart, or how many of them there are, or whether they co-exist, if we are interested in how or whether they are disposed to interact. It might also matter how they are oriented with respect to one another, or whether they are approaching each other or receding. Spatial separations, relative orientations and relative motions are typical of the properties or relations that we consider to be categorical. So if having a causal role implies being a causal power, I would readily concede that all categorical properties and relations are causal powers, just as Shoemaker, Bird and Heil all say they are. But the causal roles of such categoricals do not appear to be at all like those typical of causal powers. In my view, they are essentially different. They are different subcategories in the category of properties.

The causal powers of things vary greatly in their complexity, and their displays normally involve both instantaneous changes of state and continuing inertial processes. But at the most fundamental level, it would appear that the causal powers of things always issue

---

8. Alexander Bird defines quidditism as the thesis that there are properties (namely, the categorical ones) whose identities are independent of their causal roles. But, to define categorical properties in this way is to beg the question against them. I would define them as properties whose identities depend only on the kinds of structures they represent.

directly in instantaneous changes of state, creating new objects with new causal powers. If, for example, an atomic nucleus of atomic number n undergoes β-decay, then it ceases instantly to be a nucleus of atomic number n and becomes one of atomic number $n + 1$. It thereby acquires instantly a whole new set of causal powers, and it will continue to exist with just these new causal powers indefinitely, unless or until it in turn decays or undergoes some new and equally catastrophic change of state. At which point, the nucleus of atomic number $n + 1$ will cease to exist, and be replaced by one or more other particles each with its own new set of causal powers. And so on. Meanwhile the continuing objects themselves may move around inertially, or be propagated in the form of a Schrödinger wave, without decaying or interacting causally with anything else, thus changing their circumstances, and hence the probabilities of their undergoing various further interactions. In these complex processes the objects are always the carriers of the causal powers. But, as I understand them, the instantaneous changes of state that occur in processes of emission or absorption do not themselves have or carry causal powers. They are characterized not by what they dispose their bearers to do, but by the kinds of changes of state they realize.

If this description of basic structure of causal processes is accurate, then the causal powers displayed in instantaneous changes of state clearly have very different causal roles in nature from spatial and temporal relations between things. Here is a summary of the main differences:

(a) The instances of spatial and temporal relations cannot be located in natural objects, as the instances of causal powers always can be, because they are properties not of natural objects or events but of relations between them.

(b) There are no laws of action for spatial or temporal relations, as there are, say, of electric charge or gravitational mass. There are plenty of physical laws involving spatial and temporal relations. Indeed, all causal laws refer to spatially and temporally related events. But the spatial and temporal relations are not directly causative. They are relevant to how the powers act, and what effects they have, but they are always engaged as modifiers, never as drivers.

(c) Nothing systematic happens to things just as a result of their being separated or receding from one another. You have to know what the causal powers of the things separated are before you can say what effects, if any, or what sorts of effects, the spatial separations or rates of recession will have.

(d) Nor is there any way of triggering a spatial or temporal relation in order to make something happen as a result of two things being so related. Spatial and temporal relations would thus appear to be radically non-dispositional.

For all of these reasons I am unmoved by the threat of quidditism. A relation does not have to be a causal power to have a legitimate causal role. However, to make a good case for the position I wish to defend, it is necessary to make a detour into quantum mechanics to define a concept of physical causation, and hence of physical causal powers.

4

QUANTUM MECHANICAL REALISM[1]

Quantum mechanics has always presented a problem for scientific realists. For it does not seem to offer a coherent picture of the world. I think it does, and that there is a viable quantum mechanical model of reality. But it cannot be constructed, given the continuity constraints that we usually place on realistic models. To be a quantum mechanical realist, one has to be willing to accept that there are two fundamentally different kinds of processes occurring in nature: continuous, but quantum mechanically indeterminate, energy transfer processes and discontinuous, but spatially extended, changes of state. The unwillingness of philosophers to accept that there is such a distinction has caused many of them to doubt the reality of Schrödinger waves, and the processes of their generation and collapse. I am fully aware that I am treading on well-trodden territory, and that the technical difficulties that must be faced by anyone who is not a specialist in the field are immense. Nevertheless, I think there is a fairly clear metaphysical position on these issues derivable from the kind of essentialist realism outlined in the previous chapter, and I ask readers to bear with me.

First, realism about Schrödinger waves requires the belief that particles are always transmitted as quantum mechanically indeterminate

---

1. This chapter was written as a paper for the Philosophy of Physics seminar at the University of Adelaide in April 2008, and delivered at the Australasian Association of Philosophy Conference in Melbourne in July 2008.

waves, but always act as classically determinate particles on whatever absorbs them. The probability of absorption by a given absorbing object (e.g. measuring instrument) at a given location is determined by the value of the ψ-function at this point. Realistically, therefore, the waves must be supposed to propagate *particle realisation potentials*. Secondly, acceptance of a realistic theory of Schrödinger waves, and of the very rapid or instantaneous changes of state that quantum theory implies, commits one to the view that all transitions from indeterminate to determinate states are temporally irreversible, apparently in contradiction to the widely accepted T-symmetry thesis. Thirdly, realism about Schrödinger waves already implies a kind of non-locality, because what was spatially distributed before the event of determination suddenly becomes localized in that event. Finally, quantum realism implies that there is a common species of elementary physical causation that is probabilistic, and directed from one determinate state of affairs to another.

Schrödinger wave realism

Consider the famous "two-slit" experiment (see Figure 1): electrons, accelerated to a known energy level E, are fired from a source X through two narrow, minutely separated slits at U and L. A photographic plate is placed beyond the slits to record the positions of electrons reaching it. What happens is that an interference pattern begins to form on the plate of precisely the kind that one would expect from radiation of frequency ν, where $E = h\nu$. To those unfamiliar with quantum phenomena, probably the most surprising thing about this is that the pattern begins to take shape immediately, even when the electrons arrive at the screen very slowly, just one at a time. It is as if each electron is transmitted as a wave of frequency ν that passes through both slits. The parts of the emerging wave are then able to interfere with each other, and the pattern is the result of this interference. Yet, when the wave strikes the photographic plate, it appears to be a particle again, and the electron hits the plate at a definite point, say Y.

According to scientific realism, if, according to our best and most successful theories, a process of a certain kind appears to be occurring, then the best explanation of why this is so is that it really is

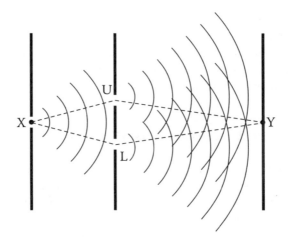

Figure 1. The two-slit experiment.

occurring, just as the theory says it is. Therefore, quantum mechanical realism requires us to be realistic about Schrödinger waves. It must be accepted that emitted particles are transmitted as waves, but do not act as waves. They act locally, just as classical particles would, and the wave amplitudes simply indicate the probabilities of their acting at one place rather then another. As far as I can see, there is only one way for scientific realists to make sense of this. They must suppose that the transmitted wave has the potential to reconstitute itself into a particle in an instant, or at least in a very short period of time, and act accordingly. The wave itself is one whose amplitude determines the probability of its being reconstituted in this kind of way at a given site of possible absorption.

However, acceptance of this account has important consequences. For it implies that there is a process of transition from a state of indeterminacy to one of determinacy (often referred to as the collapse of the wave function), which, if it occurs, does so very rapidly indeed. If it does not do so instantaneously, it certainly occurs at speeds very much greater than that of light. Therefore, the process of collapse, if it is temporally extended at all, is not one that could possibly be explained by any known dynamical laws. Therefore, the T-symmetry thesis, which applies to all mechanical processes that are fully describable classically or quantum mechanically, cannot be assumed to apply to this transition process. In fact, as we shall see very shortly, there is good reason to suppose that it does not apply to it. If this is the case, however, then the fact that the known laws of mechanics are T-symmetrical cannot possibly settle the question of whether time is essentially reversible.

T-reversibility versus T-symmetry

The essential T-reversibility and the T-symmetry theses are distinct. In his recent book, and in many places since then, Huw Price has argued for essential T-reversibility, that is, for the thesis that all events and processes occurring in the universe are essentially reversible in time. If what actually happens appears to be otherwise, he says, it is because the universe had a very low entropy past, and, consequently, changes in the direction of increasing entropy are hugely more probable than ones in the opposite direction. But the low entropy past is an accidental feature of the universe, not one of its essential properties, and we should not let this fact get in the way of a clear understanding of the nature of reality. The T-symmetry thesis is one concerning the fundamental laws of nature. If $-t$ is substituted for t uniformly throughout, it is said, the basic laws of nature all remain the same. Therefore, unless there are basic laws of a radically different kind yet to be found, there is nothing to prevent the world from evolving in the temporally reversed direction. However, the T-reversibility thesis is stronger than the T-symmetry thesis. For the T-symmetry thesis is applicable only to continually changing states of affairs. We know this, because the laws concerning such changes are the only ones that could possibly have time as a variable. Therefore, if there are any instantaneous changes of state, the T-symmetry thesis could not possibly have anything to say about whether they are T-reversible.

The case I wish to present against T-reversibility depends only on the ontology required for quantum mechanics, and the evident irreversibility of the instantaneous, or near instantaneous, process of transition from the state of indeterminacy to that of determinacy. For this process appears to have no temporal inverse. There is no known instantaneous, or nearly instantaneous, process of Schrödinger wave reflation that is at all like the reverse of the process of its collapse. Anything that absorbs a photon, electron or any other particle could plausibly re-emit a particle of the same kind from the same place. But such a re-emission would not involve the instantaneous re-emergence of a fully blown Schrödinger wave that is focused on the distant point of its eventual absorption. In fact, if we had to know where an emitted particle would eventually be absorbed in order to use Schrödinger's wave equation, we would not need it to tell us how likely it was for the particle to be absorbed here or there. A re-emitted particle would in fact be transmitted by a Schrödinger wave radiating outwards from the point of its re-emission, just as Schrödinger waves are always propagated.

I am not arguing that Schrödinger waves are not T-symmetrical. They are. If you substitute $-t$ for t, Schrödinger's equation is unaffected. But the event of energy absorption, which completes the process of energy transfer, necessarily involves the collapse[2] of the Schrödinger wave, *and it is this collapse that is temporally irreversible.* And this is so, despite the T-symmetry of the relevant law of energy transmission: Schrödinger's equation itself. We may conclude, therefore, that the event of wave absorption is temporally irreversible, even if the process of absorption is not absolutely instantaneous. To simplify the presentation, let us say that the process of transition from indeterminacy to determinacy is an "apparently instantaneous" one, and leave it an open question whether it is anything more than this.

The common characteristic of all quantum leaps is that they are apparently instantaneous. If an electron falls from one energy level to another in the process of emitting light, no one nowadays thinks that it spirals in to the lower energy level, or that there is a process by which the light gets up to speed. Maybe something is going on in the atom between its being first in an excited state and then in a less excited one. But if so, the process is not known to science. The change, to all intents and purposes, is instantaneous. The same holds for the collapse of a Schrödinger wave. The superimposed states do

---

2. I prefer the old-fashioned description of the event of absorption as a "collapse of the wavefront", because, from the point of view of a Schrödinger wave realist, this is exactly what must be supposed to occur.

not vie with each other for survival. In the event of determination, they all disappear instantly, as far as anyone can tell, except for one. And all of the energy, momentum, spin and so on that is evidently transmitted by the wave is focused at the point of absorption of the one that remains. What happens to the Schrödinger wave when it collapses is that it undergoes a quantum leap, and it is surely implausible that the mechanism for such an event, if there is one, should be governed by the familiar dynamical laws.

Therefore, if a change from a state of indeterminacy to one of determinacy occurs, there is no reason to think that this change must be T-symmetrical. Hence, there is no reason why the process of particle absorption should not be accepted just for what it appears to be: a temporally irreversible event. This is surely what a good scientific realist ought to believe. Therefore, if Schrödinger waves are physical existents, and not just convenient fictions, the case against T-reversibility would appear to be a strong one.

Alternatives to Schrödinger wave realism

There are many alternatives to Schrödinger wave realism, but none, as far as I can see, that should be acceptable to a scientific realist. The oldest, which is sometimes attributed to Niels Bohr, is the instrumentalist one. On this view, scientific theories that postulate the existence of unobservables should never be regarded as anything more than just instruments for prediction. That is, they should not be interpreted literally, as scientific realists would demand. This view that wave mechanics should be so regarded was the most widely accepted one among philosophers of science for most of the first half of the twentieth century.

A second alternative was Louis de Broglie's pilot wave theory. But it was never clear how these waves were supposed to guide the projected particle. Presumably, they steered it somehow in the direction of the path that it would have to take for it to reach the point of its eventual absorption. But, if so, how did these waves achieve this feat? In his 1952 paper, David Bohm provided a possible answer by demonstrating that a steerage mechanism was indeed possible, and that a pilot wave interpretation of Schrödinger waves could adequately be defended, if only they could be assumed to have certain causal powers, which they were not in fact known to have. Bohm's interpretation thus became known as the "hidden variable" account. To accept the kind of theory proposed by de Broglie, and also by Bohm, the probabilities calculable from the wave amplitudes of Schrödinger waves would have to be accepted as epistemic, rather than real. The difference is this: real probabilities reflect indeterminacies that are inherent in the real world; epistemic probabilities measure only our degrees of rational expectation. For example, the probability that a given neutron will decay in the next minute has an objective and precise value. It is calculable from the known half-life of the neutron. On the other hand, the probability that a particular toss of a coin will land heads is an epistemic one. It may, as things stand, be as rational to expect it to land heads as tails, but, if we really knew the values of all of the relevant variables, and all of the relevant laws of mechanical causation, and were able to do all of the necessary calculations in real time, the uncertainty of our knowledge would be replaced by a certain knowledge of the outcome. On Bohm's theory, this is the position we are in *vis-à-vis* quantum uncertainties. If only we knew the precise values of all of the relevant variables, and the precise laws of energy transmission involving these variables, we could say for certain what the outcomes of these processes would be. There is, however, no viable theory of quantum uncertainty of this kind, and none in prospect. Nor is there any guarantee that such a theory would be T-reversible, even if it were to exist.

A third possibility is Hugh Everett's (1957) many worlds theory. According to Everett, absorption events are indeed catastrophic and irreversible. But Everett does not see them as events that are destructive of real possibilities. He sees them, rather, as events of actualization. The real world, he thinks, is a multiverse, with branches splitting off from a common trunk, or from branches that have already split off from that trunk. His picture of reality is thus formally the similar Storrs McCall's "universe tree", although I do not think that he thought, as McCall does, that the branches that do not become parts of the actual world just drop off or disappear. Immediately before an event of particle absorption takes place, he says, the particle involved exists in a multitude of superimposed states, all of which are real. But at the moment of absorption, just one of them becomes actualized. At this point, the actual world splits off from the multiverse along an evolutionary path of its own. Other possible worlds, with the same history up to this time, split off in their own directions, depending on which of the superimposed states are actualized in these worlds.[3]

But Everett's theory is not one that should be acceptable to a scientific realist, even though it is realistic about all of the superimposed states occurring in energy transmission processes. It is unacceptable, because there is no sufficient reason to believe in the reality of the worlds that are not actualized. One world, the actual one, is all we need. The others may have a formal role if we are interested in developing a modal logic with a truth-functional semantics applicable to the real world.[4] But there is no need for a scientific realist to believe that all of these other worlds exist. For these other worlds have no causal explanatory roles, and the actual world would be the same, whether or not they existed. As far as I can see, the other worlds are postulated only to explain what happens to the possible states of systems that are not realized by absorption events occurring in the actual world. I think the answer to this should be that the unactualized possibilities all cease to be possible, just as the possible decay of a given neutron at $t + \partial$ ceases to be a possibility at t if the neutron actually decays at t.

A theory that may come close to the one I wish to defend is Mathias Frisch's (2000, 2005). For Frisch denies, as I do, that processes of absorption are temporal inverses of processes of emission. But Frisch's argument is much more sophisticated than mine, and I am not really able to evaluate it. Here is the quotation on which I am relying:

3. This sounds like David Lewis's "possible worlds realism". But it is importantly different from Lewis's theory. For the possible worlds in Lewis's universe are not necessarily related to each other as they are in Everett's or McCall's theories. Lewis's universe is the set of all logically possible worlds, not the set of all really possible ones.

4. See Storrs McCall, *A Model of the Universe: Space–Time, Probability, and Decision* (Oxford: Clarendon Press, 1994) for the development of such a logic.

But are absorptions really temporal inverses of emissions? For this to be true, it has to be the case that we can represent absorptions in terms of fully advanced fields. A simple model of a microscopic absorption process is the absorption of radiation by a harmonically bound charge ... . In response to an incident radiation field the charge begins to accelerate and oscillate. The field has to work against the binding force and, thus, part of the energy of the incident field is removed from the field and converted into mechanical motion of the oscillating charge. Since the charge accelerates, it not only absorbs energy, but also radiates off energy. Therefore, the effect of a microscopic absorber is partly to absorb energy and partly to re-radiate and scatter the incident field. If such an absorption process is to be the temporal inverse of an emission process, then it has to be possible to represent any contribution to the total field due to the presence of the bound change in terms of a fully advanced field. However, this is in general not possible. Since any microscopic absorber re-radiates energy, the field associated with the absorber has a component along the forward light cone of the charge and, therefore, cannot be represented as a fully advanced field. There are emissions without absorptions, but no absorptions without re-emissions.

(Frisch 2000: 398)

Frisch's argument here is not, as mine is, based on quantum mechanical realism. It is an argument from classical electrodynamics. Einstein also thought that such arguments as this could be mounted against the claim that absorptions of radiation are just the temporal inverses of emissions of radiation. "A converging spherical wave is mathematically possible", he said, "but in order to realise such a wave approximately, a tremendous number of elementary objects is needed. The elementary process of the emission of light is, thus, not reversible" (Einstein 1909: 819, Frisch's translation). Again, quantum mechanics does not come into the argument.

Price's position on quantum mechanics is derived from his essential T-reversibility thesis. But Price is fairly clearly not a quantum mechanical realist. He appears to be just an old-fashioned positivist who thinks that while quantum mechanics is empirically adequate, as any good theory must be, it can lay no claim to be descriptive of reality. This was, after all, the standard view of the nature of scientific theory at the time when quantum mechanics was being developed, and it was the view reflected in the writings of Einstein in the early years of the twentieth century. However, I think the time has come to embrace quantum mechanical realism, and consequently, to reject the idea implicit in many of Einstein's writings. The world is not, as Price supposes, essentially symmetrical in time. It is essentially asymmetrical in time, and its energy absorption processes are essentially irreversible.

The ontology of physical realism

For a physical realist, the basic existents in the world are physical systems and their physical properties and relations. By physical systems I mean causally connected structures that are causally isolated from other things. In reality, there are no such systems. For everything influences or is influenced by other things in various ways. But, in a great many cases, these influences may be ignored for the purposes of analysis or theory construction. The physical systems that exist in nature are naturally classified into kinds, and so have both essential and accidental properties. The essential properties define the natural kinds of physical systems, and the accidental properties and relations the states in which they may exist. Essentially, a physical system is understood to be any closed system that is (a) energetic (i.e. has mass or energy), (b) temporally extended and (c) intrinsically conservative of energy and all other globally conserved quantities. According to physical realism, all changes in the world are either changes concerning the physical systems that exist, or changes that occur to the states in which they exist. These changes too are naturally classified into kinds, and have both essential and accidental properties. The dynamical laws spell out the essential properties of these natural kinds of changes. Note that the ontology includes no requirement that a physical system be precisely located in space, or that it must consist entirely of systems that are. Nor is there any requirement that changes of state should take time. For a physically realistic ontology for quantum mechanics must be one that is compatible with both quantum indeterminacy, and quantum discreteness. That is, the ontology must explain why Heisenberg's indeterminacy relations must hold in every physical process. Yet it must also allow for the possibility of quantum jumps, that is, apparently instantaneous changes of state occurring within physical systems.

Quantum mechanical realism also allows us to offer a fairly precise definition of a causally connected structure. For we may define an elementary kind of process that is plausibly the essential link between the parts of all such structures. The process I have in mind is the natural sequence consisting of an emission event e_1, a single Schrödinger wave transmission process →, and an absorption event e_2. Because of the irreversibility of e_2, there is no temporal inverse of $e_1 \rightarrow e_2$. So, e_2 must occur at some time later than e_1. Let us designate such a completed process by ⇒, and call this an "elementary causal process". In general, the determinate states of physical systems that are not wholly isolated from one another may be related by elementary causal processes. But let us focus here on the different parts of the same system. Let S_A be a state of part A of the system in which, and at which time, e_1 occurs, and S_B the resulting state of part B of the system in which e_2 occurs. Then S_A and S_B must be related as elementary cause to elementary effect: $S_A \Rightarrow S_B$. In general, we may define a causally connected structure as any physical system in which all of its later determinate states are derived by this means from its earlier ones.

Consistently with the event ontology of Chapter 3, this definition allows us to be more precise about what we may consider a physical object to be. I now postulate that all natural objects consist of states of affairs that are connected by elementary causal processes. Thus quantum mechanical realism may well have some profound consequence for our theory of reality. It seems, for example, to be leading to a growing space–time worm conception of a material object, and perhaps, ultimately, to a growing block theory of the universe as a whole. However, I am getting ahead of myself.[5]

Given the ontology that I have sought to establish so far, I postulate that there are two fundamentally different natural kinds of changes that can occur in the world,[6] ones that are essentially continuing and

---

5. I shall return to develop this speculation in Chapter 6.
6. This speculation was contained in my original paper of 1987, "The Ontology of Scientific Realism", and given more prominence in *Scientific Essentialism* and in *The Philosophy of Nature* (Chesham: Acumen, 2002).

ones that are essentially discontinuous. Those that are essentially continuing are (a) inertial (i.e. will continue in the same state until terminated or otherwise changed, (b) quantum mechanically indeterministic (as Heisenberg's indeterminacy principle requires), (c) relativistic (i.e. limited by the speed of light) and (d) T-symmetric. Those that are discontinuous are apparently instantaneous (i.e. there is an inertial frame with respect to which all local changes involved in the overall change of state occur, as much as anyone can tell, at precisely the same instant). An example of the first kind is the energy transmission process that occurs when a photon or other particle is emitted from a given source. Examples of the second kind include particle emissions and wave absorptions, radioactive decays, matter/antimatter annihilations, and fissions and fusions. These changes of state are all apparently instantaneous, and there is no reason to suppose that there is any known dynamical process by which they could be brought about. The collapse of the wavefront that occurs when a Schrödinger wave is absorbed is of special interest, not only because it is apparently instantaneous, but also because it involves non-local action. If Schrödinger waves are real existents then they are spread out like waves, not localized like trajectories. Therefore, a species of non-locality must be involved in all transitions from indeterminate to determinate states.

If this account is basically correct, then it follows that, strictly speaking, there are no such things as continuously existing objects. Ordinary objects, which appear to be continuously existing, are really made up of myriads of discrete states. The continuants in reality are just Schrödinger waves of particle realization potentials. They are entities that are defined by their structures, and by the potentialities they carry. But these structures are not structures of anything. They are, as James Ladyman and Don Ross would say, just "existent structures that are not composed out of more basic entities" (2007: 155). Therefore, despite my simplistic approach, I find myself in agreement with them concerning the constitution of the strict continuants in nature. Concerning these entities, I am an "ontic structural realist". But particle emissions and absorptions are truly localized events, which, in this respect, are much more like the events of classical mechanics than the energy transmission processes that link them.

Non-locality

For historical reasons, the kind of non-locality involved in a Schrödinger wave collapse has not been as much discussed in the literature as you might expect. First, few if any of the early philosophers of quantum mechanics were Schrödinger wave realists. Consequently, they did not think of the probabilities calculable from Schrödinger's equations as anything other than epistemic ones.[7] Secondly, philosophers of quantum mechanics are generally not convinced that the process of wave collapse is strictly instantaneous. In fact, the consensus seems to be that such an event is impossible. It is not possible, it is argued, because its occurrence over a spatially extended region would not only be incompatible with the special theory of relativity, but also be too counterintuitive to be taken seriously. However, John Bell's work on the determination of the directions of spin of entangled particles has provided empirical proof that correlations between causally disconnected events do exist. So scientific realists are now being forced to rethink their attitudes, to both causality and non-locality.

A Schrödinger wave realist cannot accept that the probability of a particle's absorption at one place rather than another is just an epistemic probability. For this implies that there is an underlying determinate outcome that is unknown to us. In the early history of quantum mechanics, instrumentalism was the most widely accepted philosophy of science, and, at that time, it seemed reasonable to believe that Schrödinger waves were just scientific fictions, useful for making predictions, but not satisfactory as a guide to the nature of reality. Given an instrumentalist theory of Schrödinger waves, this would be a reasonable position to take. But the tide has now turned against instrumentalism. Philosophers of science, quite reasonably, demand explanations of the phenomena; instrumentalist theories leave them unexplained. Therefore, Schrödinger wave realism is required. Yet,

---

7. They spoke of "the probability of finding" an electron at this or that place, and they renamed Heisenberg's principle that of "uncertainty", which is a decidedly epistemic reading of Heisenberg's original "*unbestimmtheit*". "Indeterminacy" is a more neutral translation, and is the one that will be used in what follows.

belief in the kinds of things described by quantum theory, and in the causal powers that must be supposed to exist if Schrödinger wave realism is accepted, is still rare. Some scientific realists would baulk at the idea that anything that is as disseminated and transitory as a Schrödinger wave could possibly be a real existent. Many would firmly reject the claim that such an amorphous object could possibly have the propensity to manifest itself as a particle wherever the value of the ψ-function is non-zero. Most philosophers of science still seem to want ontologies of classical objects, and theories of causation as relations between classical events. But we must guard against such a nineteenth-century version of realism. If you want to be a scientific realist today, you had better be a Schrödinger wave realist. And Schrödinger wave realism already involves a commitment to non-local action.

Price has postulated the existence of backward forks (i.e. common future causes) to explain Bell's examples of non-locality, and his theory seems to have had some support from physicists. But this is an extraordinary hypothesis to account for such a simple fact. First, backward forks would not account for the apparent topological simultaneity of the correlated events. A backward fork would make it possible for simultaneous spatially separated events to occur, compatibly with the special theory of relativity. But it would not necessitate their simultaneity, unless the future event happened to be equidistant from the present simultaneous ones. The rational response, I believe, is just to accept Bell's findings at face value, and allow that spatially extended but apparently instantaneous changes of state are possible. First, one has to accept that this is possible anyway, given the non-locality of the events of Schrödinger wave absorption. Secondly, one does not need to give up the special theory of relativity to accept this obvious inference. One only has to recognize that the theories of relativity are of limited scope. They apply to all energy transfer processes, but not to instantaneous changes of state.

According to the theory of laws of nature based on the ontology of physical realism, the laws describe the essential properties of the natural kinds. Therefore, if there are two radically different kinds of changes that can occur in the world, then there must also be two radically different kinds of laws: the temporal laws that describe the essential properties of the continuing changes, and the atemporal laws that describe the essential properties of the discontinuous changes. The global laws, such as the conservation laws, must, of course, apply to all kinds of changes, continuing as well as discontinuous, since all changes of state belong to the same global category. Therefore, given this ontology, there is no requirement that the special theory of relativity should apply to discontinuous changes of state. Therefore, there is no requirement that distantly correlated events of the kind described by Bell should be proscribed. On the contrary, given Schrödinger wave realism, field-wide apparently instantaneous changes of state should be commonplace. In my view, they are. They occur wherever, and whenever, a packet of energy is absorbed. What would be surprising is to find that there are causal processes of some kind linking the correlated events, just as it would be surprising to find that there is an extended process of wave collapse, like a very fast Schrödinger wave in reverse, for instance, that culminates in the event of absorption.

The temporal laws are those apt for continuing processes, and these are agreed to be T-symmetric. They are T-symmetric, I suggest, because the relevant variable in these laws is not time, but time-interval. The atemporal laws, on the other hand, are not T-symmetric, if the time-interval required for the events they describe is strictly zero, and are not known to be T-symmetric if the time-interval is just very close to zero. Therefore, it is an open question whether the atemporal laws are T-reversible. Some may be T-reversible; others not. But if any is T-irreversible, then the T-reversibility thesis is false. I am arguing here that the kind of change that occurs when a Schrödinger wave collapses is temporally irreversible. So, my position is that the T-reversibility thesis is false.

Physical causation

I define a physical causal process as any by which a physical system gains or loses energy. An event of energy emission, for example, must be the beginning of a physical causal process that is outwardly directed, and an event of energy absorption must be the beginning of one that is directed inwardly. These processes are all likely to have direct effects and recoil effects, and set off chains of other consequential effects. Many of these must themselves be brought about by physical causal processes. Physical causal processes, I shall now argue, must all be quantum mechanically irreversible, and directed from cause to effect. I call a causal process "outwardly directed" if it is initiated by the emission of a particle in the form of a Schrödinger wave. Such waves, being inertial, will continue indefinitely, or until terminated in an event of absorption. Let us call the effect that the wave collapse then has on the system that absorbs it its "direct effect".

From the point of view of the system that is directly affected, the causation is inwardly directed. For it now has to adjust to the increase in mass or energy that the system has acquired. The receiving system may then do any of a large number of things, depending on the energy and nature of what has been transmitted, and the nature of the system that has been directly affected. It may, for example, go into an excited state, be annihilated, become ionized or even undergo fission. Inevitably, there will be many knock-on effects of absorptions. New emissions are likely to result, and new absorptions to occur in consequence of these.

But this is only half of the story. For, necessarily, all emissions also affect the systems they leave behind. And these systems must adjust to the losses of energy or mass they have thereby sustained. An atom with atomic number n, for example, that loses an electron through β-decay, will cease to be one of the kind it was, and become an atom with atomic number $n + 1$. If it loses mass through α-radiation, then its atomic number will be reduced by two, and its atomic weight by approximately four. And this change of state may then set off processes of change that ramify through the surrounding systems. Let us call these collectively the "recoil effects" of the original emission.

The elementary causal relationship between the states S_A and S_B that may be established by the elementary causal process $\Rightarrow$ is one that holds between determinate states of affairs. It is temporally directed, and intrinsically conservative of energy and all of the other globally conserved quantities. Therefore, it has precisely the kinds of properties that we should expect to find in such a basic relationship. I speculate that all physical causal relationships between systems can be understood as combinations of these elementary ones.

Given this theory, it follows that the relations between physical causes and their effects are generally probabilistic, even if macroscopic causal relationships seldom appear to be so. For the event of elementary causation (i.e. the emission of energy) is never an absolute guarantee that the elementary effect (the event of absorption) will occur when and where it does. All we can say for certain is that, other things being equal, it is most likely to occur where the Schrödinger wave is most intense. And this is not just for lack of knowledge. For if one is a realist about Schrödinger waves, one has to believe in indeterminacy, and believe that the probabilities calculable from the values of the ψ-function are measures of realization potentials, which are real dispositional properties.

Quantum realism and entropy theory

In general, the direction of entropy increase depends on the probabilities of the various possible states of the systems under consideration. Therefore, if we wish to gauge the effect, if any, of the temporal irreversibility of elementary causal processes on entropy, we have to consider how this asymmetry affects relationships between states of affairs. Let $S_A \Rightarrow S_B$ be any elementary causal relationship that happens to exist between the states S_A and S_B of the systems A and B. The question to be considered is whether the fact that this relationship holds in this direction implies that the converse relationship $S_B \Rightarrow S_A$ could not possibly hold. I think the answer is that it does not. For there might well be a determinate causal relationship $S_B \Rightarrow S_A$. But, if there is such a causal relationship, it cannot be one that is based on the temporal mirror image of the underlying causal process, because there is no such thing. That is, the elementary causal process that would establish $S_B \Rightarrow S_A$ cannot be just the temporal mirror image of the elementary causal process that established $S_A \Rightarrow S_B$.

To convince yourself of this, consider once again the two-slit experiment described above (p. 75). The question is whether there could be an emission event occurring at Y on the photographic plate that produces a pair of Schrödinger waves, one focused on the slit U and the other on L, but out of phase just enough for them to be in phase when they reach their respective destinations, and then, on passing through the slits, blossoming out into a single Schrödinger wave focused on the original source of emission X, where it is finally absorbed. This is not possible. Therefore, a temporal mirror image of the elementary causal process that established $S_A \Rightarrow S_B$ in the first place is not possible. However, we know that $S_B \Rightarrow S_A$ could occur, because the angle of refraction through the slits would be the same for a Schrödinger wave returning from the original point of absorption and proceeding back to the original point of emission. So there must be a possible elementary causal process that would ground such a relationship. And of course there is. It is just a normal Schrödinger wave emitted at the original point of absorption. This process is not, however, a *temporal* mirror image of the original process; it is a *spatial* mirror image of it. For it is just an elementary causal process, which, in this case is going from right to left, not one that is the temporal mirror image of the original process. Whether all elementary determinate causal relationships of this kind are spatially reversible, I do not know. Perhaps they are. But, if so, their reversibility has nothing to do with the T-symmetry of the Schrödinger wave. It has to do only with S-symmetry (i.e. spatial symmetry). Indeed, you would get the same result, even if Schrödinger's equation was not T-symmetric. Therefore, the T-symmetry of $\rightarrow$, and the T-irreversibility of the underlying causal process are both irrelevant to the question of whether $S_A \Rightarrow S_B$ is T-reversible, and the standard argument that $S_A \Rightarrow S_B$ must be T-symmetric because $\rightarrow$ is T-symmetric is invalid.

In general, for a system consisting of atoms in the states S_1 and S_2 to be in thermodynamic equilibrium, the number m of atoms in the state S_1 would have to be in balance with the number n in the state S_2. If m/n were greater than this number, then, other things being equal, the system would tend to change in such a way as to reduce this ratio. The T-symmetry or otherwise of the energy transfer processes required to adjust this ratio is irrelevant to the calculation.

Quantum and causal realism

Quantum mechanical realism implies physical causal realism. For if Schrödinger waves are real and directed, then elementary causal processes are real and directed, and determinate causal processes linking determinate states of affairs are real and directed. Therefore, unless there are energy transfer processes of kinds we do not know about, all causal processes linking determinate states of affairs are real and directed. Therefore, philosophers of science need not be reluctant, as many are, to talk of causation as a real and directed physical process. Russell once remarked that scientists do not talk much about causes: the laws of physics, he said, are mostly functional correlations. And, according to many philosophers, causal talk is second-grade discourse, useful for plumbers and diagnosticians, but of little use to scientists, except perhaps when their apparatus appears to be faulty, or they are wanting to know why their paper has been rejected. They think of it as second-grade discourse, because of (a) the pernicious influence of Hume, who psychologized it, and (b) the widespread belief that the causal order depends on the temporal order, which in turn depends either on the direction entropy increase, or on how human beings process information.

However, if Schrödinger wave realism is accepted, physical causal processes are real and temporally directed, and their temporal directedness has nothing to do with the direction entropy increase, or with human psychology. It has to do only with the irreversibility of physical causal processes. Of course, it is a trivial semantic convention which direction we say is earlier or later, and naturally we choose the direction that accords best with common usage. But having chosen the direction of the expanding Schrödinger wave as future-directed, there is an underlying fact of the matter whether S_A occurs before S_B, or conversely. It has nothing to do with how we perceive it.

.

5

CAUSAL POWERS AND
CATEGORICAL DIMENSIONS

Ideally, physical systems are causally connected structures that are causally isolated from other things. There is no good reason to believe that there are any physical systems that are really isolated in this way. But this does not matter, since we are usually able to abstract from the actual circumstances of things to consider how they would be in themselves, and so discuss their various properties. The problem of abstraction becomes more difficult the smaller or more diffuse the objects we are concerned with. For then, the identities of objects are less well defined. But, in this chapter we shall be concerned with the properties of ordinary middle-sized things, without regard to these difficulties. In the kinds of cases to be discussed, they hardly arise.

It will be argued here that there are two essentially different kinds of properties of physical systems. There are properties whose natures are dispositional, and ones whose natures are structural. The former are often grouped together as "causal powers", and the latter as "categorical properties". But I do not much like this way of classifying properties, because it suggests, wrongly in my view, that dispositionality is a sufficient condition for causality. The causal powers are just a proper subset of the dispositional properties, and will be discussed as such.

To facilitate discussion of these two kinds of properties, it will be helpful to introduce, at the outset, the concept of a dimension. Dimensions, as I shall explain presently, are respects in which things may be the same or different. The quantities, for example, are all dimensions. For two things can be the same in respect of any quantity if and only if there could also be things that are different in this respect. Most of the properties that we call "causal powers" are quantities, and are therefore dimensions by this criterion. Let us call them "causal dimensions". The same is true of most of the properties we call "categorical", although many of them are not quantitative. Thus, two things can be the same shape, and they can also be of different shape. Let us use parallel terminology, then, and call them "categorical dimensions". The issue to be discussed in this chapter is whether there is an essential difference between the categorical and causal dimensions of things and, if so, whether either could exist in the world as we know it without the other. It will be argued here that the causal dimensions could not exist at all if there were no categorical ones. For there could not possibly be an instance of a causal dimension that had no location, and location, as we shall see, cannot be defined except with reference to the categorical dimensions of things. Consequently, the causal dimensions of things are ontologically dependent on the categorical ones. It will also be argued that the categorical dimensions are epistemically dependent on the causal ones. For without them the world would be unknowable. Therefore, things must have both categorical and the causal dimensions, if their existence is to be both possible and knowable.

The argument depends crucially on acceptance of a realistic metaphysics of physical causation of the kind outlined in Chapter 4. For, if we proceed intuitively, it is relatively easy to make a case that some categorical properties have causal powers. One can argue, for example, that since the shape of a person causes the shape of her image in the mirror, her shape is a causal power. There is no denying that reflection in a mirror is a causal process, or that existence of the reflective image is a result of this process. But the shape is not, metaphysically speaking, a causal power, as causal powers will here be understood. For it is not a source of energy transmission processes, or a power to resist the forces due to such processes. Nor is there a law of action of shape. For shape is, rightly, not considered to be anything that characteristically does anything. The causal powers involved in this case are just the sources of the light that illuminates the body, the powers of the body's surface or clothing to reflect light of various wavelengths, and the special reflective powers of the mirror involved.

Dimensions and their values

In *Scientific Essentialism* (2001), I used the term "generic universals" to refer to most of the things that I now wish to call "dimensions". It is true that for every generic universal there is a dimension. But I now think that to describe them as "generic universals" is misleading. For generic universals are more fundamental than classical ones, and, in general, the more specific a species, the less fundamental it is ontologically. First, if the quantity q did not exist, then no specific value, say q_0, of q could be instantiated. Therefore, the instantiation of any specific value of a quantity presupposes the existence of that quantity. Secondly, the quantity q cannot be constituted by its instantiated values alone. For many of the values of q may never be instantiated. Therefore, quite apart from all of the usual objections to disjunctive universals, the quantity q cannot plausibly be regarded as a disjunctive universal the elements of which are the specific universals corresponding to the instantiated values of q. The same holds for dimensions. Dimensions are ontologically more significant than any of their species or values, and in the end it often does not matter which, if any, of the specific values of the dimensions are instantiated.

According to Fred Dretske, Michael Tooley and David Armstrong's well-known theory of laws of nature, laws are contingently necessary relations between universals. But, if by universals, these philosophers mean classical universals, then this is plainly false. For the required relations between the universals must, in nearly all cases, be relations between quantities, not only between specific values of these quantities. The latter would be just instances of the laws, relevant only to the specific values of the variables in those laws that are instantiated. And, the laws themselves would not be expressible as relations between universals, unless the universals in question were generic. Moreover, if the instantiations of the laws were regarded as the fundamental ones, then all of these postulated relations between the universals would have to be regarded as distinct sets of relations, and the laws themselves as mere generalizations over them. But, if that were the case, then the whole point of Dretske, Tooley and Armstrong's analysis would be lost. For the laws would then be just empirical generalizations over known cases, and so, for a Humean, of no interest to those researchers who have to consider new cases. For a decent account of laws of nature, we should have to regard them as expressing contingent relations of natural necessitation between generic universals, not classical ones. I do not so regard them, of course, because I do not believe that there really are any contingent relations of natural necessitation.

To avoid confusion, and to better reflect the nature of reality, the language we use to describe properties should reflect the ontological standing of the different kinds of universals. And, if we have to make this change anyway, then I think we had better make it in the best way we can. There is no need for us to be bound by any of the ancient traditions. Dimensions, as I understand them, are more or less general natural respects in which things may be the same or different. They are like generic universals in some ways, since they have essences and species. But, as I think of them, they are subtly different. Here is how I define the relevant concepts:

1. An *infimic species* of a property or natural kind D is any species of D that has no subspecies.
2. Two things are *specifically the same in respect of* D if and only if the instances of D in or of these things are members of the same infimic species of D.
3. D is a *dimension* if and only if:
(a) D is a natural property or kind;
(b) there is an x and y, $x \neq y$, that are specifically the same in respect of D; and
(c) there is an x and y that are specifically different in respect of D.
4. An *actual value* of D is any infimic species of D.
5. A *value* of D is any possible infimic species of D.

In contrast,

A *classical universal* U exists if and only if:
(a) U is a natural property or kind;

(b)   there is at least one thing that has U;

(c)   it is possible for more than one thing to have U; and

(d)   everything that has U is specifically the same in respect of U.
      A *generic universal* GU exists if and only if GU is like a classical universal, except that not everything that has GU is specifically the same in respect of GU.

The infimic species of generic universals are necessarily universals, and universals, as we normally understand them, are Aristotelian, that is, they exist if and only if they are instantiated. But dimensions are conceptually different from generic universals. First, dimensions may have other dimensions as species. The dimension of shape, for example, has the dimension of polyhedrality as a species. For every possible polyhedron has a shape, but not every shape is polyhedral. Secondly, dimensions have what I call "values". These values include all of the infimic species of all of the kinds of things that are alike in respect of the dimensions in question. These are what we may call the instantiated values of the dimensions. But as I and, I imagine, most scientists and mathematicians would wish to conceive of them, the values of the dimensions need not all be instantiated. Indeed, it is one of the strengths of the concept of a dimension that dimensions may have values that are not actual values.

Consider the set of all polyhedra. Membership of this set is not thought to be limited to the values of the dimension of polyhedrality that are actually instantiated. The set that everyone has in mind is naturally the wider one: the set of all possible polyhedra. It is important, therefore, that we should acknowledge at once that many of the ultimately specific values of the dimensions may not be instantiated. And the simplest way of doing this is to concede that the values of the dimensions may not always be Aristotelian universals. But clearly, they are still universals of some kind. For the only thing that distinguishes them from the instantiated values of the dimensions is just that they are not necessarily instantiated. They are what most philosophers would recognize at once as Platonic universals. They have essences, just as Aristotelian universals do. They also have well-defined positions in the natural hierarchies of universals. Clearly, the concepts of dimensions and their values are important in mathematics. We shall return to consider their significance for this field in the following chapter. I introduce them here because I think that they are also important in the sciences, where all, or nearly all, of the important property concepts are dimensions.

Two kinds of properties

The properties that we think of as causal powers are of a number of different kinds. There are properties, such as the power of one negatively charged particle to repel another, that are straightforwardly causal powers. For the displays of these powers are paradigmatically causal processes involving energy transmissions. There are others that we think of as capacities, which seem to have a different nature. Inertial mass, for example, measures the power of a body to resist acceleration by a given force. This capacity is certainly a dispositional property, and is plausibly a power of some kind. But a display of the inertial mass of a body A does not involve any emission of energy from A. On the contrary, A has to be a recipient of transmitted energy for this capacity to be manifested, and its measured value for a given force is inversely proportional to the acceleration induced in A. Then again, there are reciprocal capacities that we call causal powers. The capacity of sugar to dissolve in water, for example, would seem to be just the same thing as the capacity of water to dissolve sugar. There is clearly causation (energy transmissions) of some kind involved in this process, but no obvious directionality to it. This may be more appearance than reality. A fourth kind of so-called "causal power" is the class of propensities. Propensities are certainly dispositional properties. For the instability of a particle, or the disposition of a radioactive substance to decay in one way rather than another, is, like any disposition, one of a kind that could, in principle, never be manifested. But, properly understood, it is not a causal power. For there is no good reason to think that events of radioactive decay are physically caused by anything, or that they are themselves physical causal processes.

In sum, we may say that causal powers are the sources of physical changes due to energy transfer processes, or of resistance to the forces that would produce such changes, or to some combination of these. In what follows it will be argued that some, but not all, of the properties in nature have one such characteristic, and therefore that some, but not all, of the properties in nature are causal powers. Of those that are not causal powers, most are among the categorical dimensions of things, that is, they are properties whose essences are purely relational or structural. But the changes due to collapsing wavefronts and radioactive decay processes, which make determinate what was previously indeterminate, are evidently uncaused. Therefore, the half-lives of radioactive substances, and the realization potentials of Schrödinger waves are neither categorical properties nor causal powers. They belong to a third, and metaphysically interesting, category. But they will not be discussed here.

To gauge the effect of any causal power P, it is necessary to consider what would happen if it, and it alone, were absent. Let E_0 be the outcome that would exist in the absence of P, and E the actual outcome. Then the difference $E - E_0$ must be the measure of the effect of the operation of P. In general, P will be a causal dimension of the set-up S, and the changes it induces and/or prevents in the circumstances will depend on the value of P. Let P_0 be the value of P for S. If P is what I am calling a "causal power", then P must have a law of action A that describes what it does when it acts. For, if there were no such law, there would be nothing to connect different exercises of the same causal power. Since, by hypothesis, the value of the causal power involved here in transforming E_0 into E is P_0, the law of action $A(P, x)$ for P must be one that has the effect $E - E_0$, where $P = P_0$, and $x = E_0$. That is, $E - E_0 = A(P_0, E_0)$. This effect, it will be noted, is a function of two variables, P_0, which is the value of the dimension of the causal power in the circumstances, and E_0, which is the set of values of the relevant dimensions of the circumstances in which P is operating.

The position that I wish to defend is that there are two essentially different kinds of dimensions involved in all causal processes: the categorical ones required for the characterization of E and E_0, and the causal ones for the definitions of P and P_0. The categorical dimensions are the so-called "categorical properties", and the causal dimensions are the so-called "causal powers".

To illustrate, let E describe some apparatus that includes: a perfect lens B, a thin object A placed to its left at a distance l_1 along the principal axis of the lens, and a screen C vertical to this axis at a distance

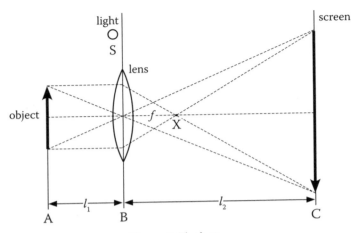

Figure 2. The lens.

l_2 to the right of the lens. Let f be the focal length of the lens, and suppose that l_1 and l_2 satisfy the equation:

L_1
$$1/l_2 + 1/l_1 = 1/f$$

Suppose now that the whole apparatus is currently illuminated by a single light S, which shines on A, but not on C. Then, a clear inverted image of A on C should now be observable, the size M of which is magnified (or diminished) by the factor l_2/l_1 (see Figure 2). That is, there is a law of magnification:

L_2
$$M = l_2/l_1$$

Let E_0 be the situation that exists when the lens B is removed. Then $E - E_0$ consists of the lens in place and the inverted image on the screen. And the laws L_1 and L_2 will together constitute the law of action of the imaging power of the lens. Note that the variables in this law of action are all categorical properties: distances, focal lengths, sizes, orientations and magnifications. The only causal powers involved are those of the lens, the air in which the apparatus is built, the source of light and the reflective powers of the materials of the object A and the screen C. So, in this case at least, the law of action of the causal power involved, that is, the imaging power of the lens, is a function from one set of categorical properties to another.

It would be neat if I could say that the laws of action of the causal powers were all like this, involving only the categorical dimensions of the causal set-ups. But this is not so. For there are various kinds of positive and negative feedback mechanisms that can directly affect the values of the powers involved in their operation. Thus, the power of a battery to light a torch bulb will diminish with use, and do so because of its use. On the other hand, the capacity of a mouse to run a maze will increase with practice, and will do so because of this practice. So it would be wrong to assume that the causal powers of things cannot be changed by their action, or by the action of other causal powers. Nevertheless, I do not believe that there are any causal powers that have laws of action that are independent of where these powers are spatiotemporally located *vis-à-vis* the things on which they act. Therefore, the laws of action of the powers must always specify where the active powers are located.

So, the position that I wish to defend is this: there are two essentially different kinds of properties involved in all causal processes – the categorical ones required for the descriptions of E and E_0, and the causal ones for the descriptions of P and P_0. This position has been attacked on two fronts. There are strong categoricalists, who deny that there are any genuine causal powers, and strong dispositionalists, who deny that there are any real categorical properties. I have discussed the principal arguments for strong categoricalism at length elsewhere. There is, however, one issue, initially raised by Armstrong, that remains controversial, namely, Armstrong's argument that belief in causal powers involves an unacceptable form of Meinongianism. I shall have something to say about this in the following section. But the main objection to my position now appears to be coming from the strong dispositionalists, who argue (a) that if the categorical properties of things had no causal powers then we should not know about them, and (b) that if the causal powers of the different categorical properties were not distinctive of them then we should have no way of distinguishing between them. Therefore, they say, the categorical properties must all have or be distinctive causal powers, that is, powers that would distinguish them essentially from one another. Otherwise, it is said, they would be mere quiddities. I call this "the argument from quidditism".

The Meinongian argument

In my "Essentialism and Natural Kinds", I argued that the tropes of causal powers are not fundamentally different from those of other properties. For the tropes of all genuine properties are the relationships of "bearing" that hold between the things that have these properties and the universals of which these tropes are instances. Thus, the difference between a trope of a causal power, and one of any other kind of property, lies in the nature of the universal that is instantiated in its bearer. A trope of triangularity, for example, is a relationship between an object and a tropic universal (i.e. triangularity). And a trope of the causal power of a substance to dissolve sugar is an instance of the relationship between that substance (e.g. the tea in the teacup) and the dynamic natural kind, which is of the causal process of dissolving sugar. Therefore, if one believes in dynamic universals, as I do, then one should have no difficulty in believing that there are tropes of causal powers, such as that of having the power to dissolve sugar, even if some of these powers are never displayed.

A dynamic universal is like any other universal; it exists if any instance of it exists. Therefore, a natural kind of process exists if any instance of it does. If the process is of a generic kind, then it exists if any instance of any species of it exists. That is all: it does not require that every, or any particular, species of that generic kind of process should exist. Nor does it depend on whether any instance of it involving the objects or substances in question exists. Therefore, the existence of a trope of a causal power in an object has nothing to do with whether it has ever exercised this power. It depends only on whether the dynamic universal that is the natural kind of process in question exists, which is a very different matter.

The natural kind of process that is the dissolving of a substance of one kind in one of another kind certainly exists. Therefore, the relationship of solute-to-solvent also exists. And this relationship, I contend, is a universal: one that is borne by sugar and water respectively as relata, and by many other pairs of substances of different kinds. So, even if one does not believe in dynamic universals, one does not need to embrace Meinongianism to explain the truth of the causal conditional "If this lump of sugar were placed in water, it would dissolve". If the fact that a billiard ball has the relationship of bearing to a universal, namely, roundness, is one that necessitates that the ball is round, why should an ordered pair of objects, such as a lump of sugar and a cup of water, not be a bearer of the solute-to-solvent relationship? And, if they are the bearers of this relational universal, why should this fact not itself necessitate the lump's having the potential to dissolve in the water? And, if it does necessitate the lump's having this potential, why should the sugar cube's standing with water in the relationship of solute-to-solvent not be considered to be the truthmaker for the proposition that if this lump of sugar were to be immersed in the water, then it would dissolve?

Armstrong (1999a) has objected to this causal power analysis of solubility on the ground that it implies the existence of mere possibilia. In particular, he says that if causal powers are inherent properties that support counterfactual conditionals, then these properties must somehow "point to" the consequents of these conditionals. And this, he thinks, poses a special problem for any causal powers that may never be exercised. In these cases, he says, the displays never occur, and the consequents are never realized. Therefore, anything that is the bearer of an unmanifested disposition must somehow "point to" a non-existent, but presumably possible, object. A property's "pointing to" a non-existent object, he says, is a Meinongian attribute. Therefore, he argues, anyone who embraces dispositional realism, as I do, must also be willing to accept this form of Meinongianism. I do not.

Armstrong's argument appears to depend on his acceptance of a "possible worlds" analysis of the truth conditions for causal conditionals. For the truthmaker theory of such conditionals does not mention any mere possibilities. There is, according to me, a natural kind of process of dissolving, and hence a natural kind of relationship of solute-to-solvent. These are facts about the actual world. It is also a fact about the actual world that sugar and water stand in this relationship. Therefore, the proposition that if sugar is placed in water it will dissolve is straightforwardly true. It corresponds to what actually exists. Possibilities do not come into it. In my view, the truthmakers for causal conditionals are the natural kinds of relationships implied by the existence of natural kinds of causal processes and the relationships of bearing between the subjects of these conditionals and these natural kinds of relationships. The Meinongian objection to the existence of unmanifested, and never to be manifested, causal powers is therefore misguided.

Quidditism

Bird (2005) has distinguished between strong and weak versions of dispositional essentialism, and argued for Shoemaker's (1980) strong version. He identified the strong version as the claim that what makes a property the property it is, that is, what determines its identity, is its potential for contributing to the causal powers of the things that have it. Bird's case for the strong version was that anything weaker would condemn us to quidditism. For if there were any property whose identity did not depend on what it disposed its bearer to do, but only on what it was (quidditism), then we should, necessarily, be ignorant of it.

Shoemaker's claim that the identity of a property must depend on what it disposes its bearer to do has to be understood as an ontological thesis if it is to be relevant here. We might grant him that to describe the properties of things we must observe them, if they are directly observable, or be able to infer their existence from what we can directly observe, if they are not. Hence, we might agree that if a property is not observable, and has no role in determining what happens in any realizable circumstances, then we should, necessarily, be ignorant of it. But this is compatible with causal powers and other kinds of properties having essentially different kinds of causal roles. It is also, perhaps surprisingly, compatible with quiddities being directly observable.

According to the analysis of causal powers given above (§ "Two kinds of properties"), the law of action of a causal power P necessarily has the form $E - E_0 = A(P, x)$, where E is the actual outcome, E_0 is what the outcome would have been in the absence of the causal power, and x is the set of circumstances existing at the time and place where the power is activated. In this equation, the effect of the causal power's action, $E - E_0$, is a function of both the specific value of the power, and of the values of the dimensions of the circumstances of its operation. These dimensions may indeed include some causal ones. But there is no reason at all why they should all be causal dimensions. On the contrary, there is every reason to think that the categorical dimensions of place and time are necessarily involved in every law of action of a causal power. For it would indeed be a very strange causal power if its effect on a given object were independent of where or when it acted. To this it may be objected that place and time are not natural properties, which is a moot point. But whether we count place and time as themselves being natural properties does not matter. Place and time can only be defined in terms of spatial and temporal relationships, and these certainly are dimensions. Moreover, a thing's spatial and temporal relationships to other things are undoubtedly respects in which it may be the same as, or different from, other things. So there is no harm in speaking of spatiotemporal location as a dimension.

The question of whether quiddities are observable may seem like a nonsense question. For how could anything that does not have any effects essentially be observable? My answer is straightforward. Easily. For it could certainly do so accidentally. The shape of an object has no effects essentially (since it does not by itself do anything), but it may well have effects accidentally, depending on the circumstances in which the object is placed. An unilluminated square has no visible effects. But an illuminated square does have such effects. It looks square. It is true that it does not have this effect essentially. For it is not essential to the squareness of an illuminated object that it should look square to human beings, or even that we should be capable of vision. Squareness in itself is not a source of energy transfer processes. Nor does it act to resist any forces produced by such processes. It is just a quiddity.

Biochemists spend a great deal of time constructing molecules, in the hope that some of them may turn out to be useful. The process is one that involves making substitutions for atoms or radicals in molecular structures that are already known to them. They know from experience what substitutions are possible, how to make them, which are likely to be successful and hence what the structure of the molecule they are building is likely to be. They may also have some idea of what its properties will be. But there is no reason to suppose that the identities of these molecules depend on what these properties turn out to be. Their identities depend on what substitutions have actually been made in the laboratory. And, plausibly, they may not know this for years. Indeed, they may never know it. Therefore,

Shoemaker's thesis that the identity of a molecule depends essentially on what it disposes its bearer to do is plainly false. For the identity of a molecule depends on that of its structure, and the identity of the structure of a molecule depends essentially on what it is, not on what it does. In Bird's terminology, it is a quiddity.

The biochemist's aims in constructing a new kind of molecule were presumably to discover its dispositional properties, for example whether it will make a better treatment for some disease than any other similarly composed or structured molecules. Does it kill bugs as effectively? Does it have nasty side effects? Do some people react strongly to it? Does it have any long-lasting effects on patients? Naturally, the investigators will also want to confirm that the molecule they have constructed has the structure they think it has. And there are many techniques for doing this that have been perfected over the years. But the molecule exists, and has its essential structural properties independently of what these techniques may reveal. Of course, the confirmation process presupposes that the molecular structure affects its physical and chemical properties in various ways, as verified by experiments in X-ray crystallography, treatment with other chemicals and so on. But all of these facts are likely to have been established quite independently of the properties of the molecule under investigation. In any case, the molecule will have the structure it has, and would still have this structure, even if no techniques had ever been discovered for confirming that it is what the biochemists think it is.

If the structural properties of some molecules are quiddities, which seems clearly to be true, then it is reasonable to suppose that all molecular structures have identities that depend essentially on what they are, rather than on what they do. Therefore, to deal with the facts of chemistry, we need an ontology that includes some non-dispositional properties. However, the causal powers and other dispositional properties of molecules can never be derived just from their structures. For how molecules of a given kind are disposed to behave must depend not only on the specific locations within the structures of the various kinds of atoms that constitute them, but also on the dispositional properties of these atoms. Any dispositional properties that depend in this way on the underlying atomic structures of molecules will naturally be essential to them. But they still have to be discovered.

Dispositional properties and categorical structures

The intuitive distinction that most philosophers are inclined to make between categorical and dispositional properties is plausibly grounded in their essentially different character. Dispositional properties depend on what things are disposed to do. Categorical properties depend on the structures that things have, or the relations they bear to other things, independently of how they might be disposed to behave. The question we must now ask is: how are these two very different kinds of properties related?

The shape of an object can be revealed to us by sight. Or, it may be revealed to us by touch. Let P be the set of relevant causal powers operating in the first kind of case, and Q the set of relevant causal powers operating in the second kind of case. Let E_0 be the state of affairs that would have existed in the absence of anyone either looking or touching the object in question. (In this case, the shape of the object would be unaffected.) Let $E_p - E_0$ be the effect of Fred looking at the object, and $E_Q - E_0$ be the effect of Freda touching it. Then E_p and E_Q must both include knowledge of the object's shape. But the effects, which are $E_p - E_0$ and $E_Q - E_0$ respectively, do not include any changes to the shape. It remains the same throughout the process. Therefore, to suppose that the shape of the object was itself a causal power responsible for Fred and Freda acquiring their knowledge of it is to suppose that the object has a causal power that is capable of delivering such an effect without itself being changed by it. This is contrary to the metaphysical principle of *causa aequat effectum*, which was used with devastating critical effect by Robert Mayer in developing his early version of the law of conservation of energy. It is also an assumption that, if true, would render the causal powers that actually affected Fred's and Freda's senses irrelevant to the process.

Suppose that the thing is circular. Then Fred and Freda must both have come to know (by feeling and touching respectively) that it is circular. But the causal powers that led to Fred and Freda acquiring this knowledge were essentially very different from each other, and neither of them included the shape. For the shape acted only to determine where the relevant causal powers were. It did not act in their stead. One way of acquiring the knowledge depended on the capacity of the object to reflect light; the other depended on its resistance to pressure. Of course, if the shape of the object had been different, then the specific locations of these powers would have been different. Or, if the lighting or circumstances had been different, then the values of these powers would have been different. But essentially the same causal powers would have been involved in acquiring the knowledge, depending on which method of observation had been used.

My claim that there are categorical properties as well as dispositional ones is rejected by strong dispositionalists, mainly because they think that to postulate the existence of properties that are not, or do not have, causal powers is to envisage properties that have no causal roles, and which, therefore, we are incapable of knowing about. But this is where they go wrong. For, as I understand them, causal powers and categorical properties both have causal roles. Their roles are just radically and essentially different. The causal powers are the driving forces. The categorical properties only determine the locations or distributions of the these forces, and ultimately, the directions, speeds, accelerations, changes of shape and other specific effects of these forces. Our acquisition of knowledge of shape is one of these other specific effects. It is not caused by the shape itself, but by the ways in which the causal powers of the object being observed are distributed over the object in question. The shape is not itself a causal power. For it is not distributed over the object in the way that the capacities of the object to resist pressure and to reflect light are distributed. The surface of a sphere is not everywhere spherical. But a hard surface is everywhere hard, and a white one is everywhere white.

The causal powerlessness of categorical properties

There is a powerful argument that locations are not causal powers. It is this:

1. Every instance of every causal power must have some location.
2. Two different instances of the same causal power cannot have the same location.

3. Therefore, if location were a causal power, every instance of location would have some location, and no two distinct instances of the same location could have the same location.
4. But this is absurd.

An instance of location *is* a location. It is not something that *has* a location.

5. Therefore, locations are not causal powers.

This argument may easily be extended:

6. The locations of the powers determine where, when and on what they may act. How is this possible?
7. Is it possible because the actual locations of things really do have causal powers?
8. No. The things located at particular places have causal powers. But the locations do not have causal powers, because, if you take the things away, the locations remain, but the causal powers cease to be there.
9. Therefore, the locations of things do not have, any causal powers.
10. Therefore, from 5 and 9, the locations of things neither are, nor have, any causal powers.

If this argument is sound, and I believe it is, then it follows that locations are all quiddities. But there is no doubt whatsoever that where the causal powers are located makes the world of difference to what happens. Therefore, locations can affect the outcomes of causal processes, and even determine which causal processes can occur, without themselves being or having causal powers. But, if this is the case, then the same must be true of all of the categorical dimensions involved in defining locations. Moreover, there are easily constructed extensions to this argument that establish just as conclusively that shape, orientation, handedness and other categorical properties are causally powerless. And, therefore, we may reasonably conclude that all of the standard examples of categorical properties are essentially causally powerless. Therefore, they are all quiddities.

The problem of knowledge of categorical dimensions

The claim that the categorical dimensions and structures of things are all quiddities, that is, properties that do not have causal powers essentially, is bound to be controversial. The same is true of the claim that our knowledge of these dimensions and structures is through the accidental properties or circumstances of the things that have these dimensions or structures, or of ourselves as observers. But, on reflection, it is not really so surprising. A 3D camera makes a 3D image of its field of vision. It transforms every visible shape in its field of vision into a similar shape within the visual image it forms. But the visible shapes are not the causes of the shapes in the visual image. For they do not do anything other than determine the boundaries of the objects that have these shapes, and therefore the possible loci of the light reflectors. It is true that if the shapes did not exist, a visual image of these shapes would not be formed. But it is also true that if the light or the camera did not exist, there would be no visual image of anything. Therefore, the imaging process requires both kinds of properties. Without the shapes, there would be nothing to represent visually; without the causal powers, there would be no means of observing the environment or representing it pictorially.

In common parlance, we may say that the shapes of the objects being photographed or observed cause the shapes of the visual images that are produced, the shapes of the patterns of radiation on our retinas, or the shapes of the encoded images in our visual cortices. But we must not be fooled by this. The shapes of the objects are not the sources of the energy transmissions that result in these other shapes. They are not causal powers. They are just some of the categorical dimensions of the objects in view. The sources of the energy transmissions that create the images, and the patterns on our retinas and in our brains, are the lights by which the objects are illuminated, the lenses of our cameras or in our eyes that focus the light, or the light sensitivities of the rods and cones on our retinas. These are the causal powers. The shapes of the objects determine only the shapes of the surfaces that reflect the light. They do not cause these surfaces to exist, or to have the shapes they have, as they would if they were genuine causes of these things.

The case for accepting the categorical dimensions and structures of things as quiddities thus depends on our having a realistic theory of causation. For if one had no such theory, it would be easy to confuse preconditions with causes, the categorical properties of pre-existing states of affairs with causal powers, and the categorical properties of the resulting states of affairs with the effects of these supposed powers. A realist about causal powers cannot accept any theory of causation that would allow such confusion. Obviously, Hume's regularity theory is ruled out. What is required is a metaphysical theory of causal processes that develops an adequate theory of the basic causal mechanisms in nature, and of the characteristics of the relata of causal relationships. This was one of the projects of Chapter 4, where it was argued that causal processes are essentially energy transmission processes whose initial and final states are categorical states of affairs. And this is exactly what we see in the photographic and visual examples that we have been discussing.

Chemical laws relating to structurally defined entities

If, as I have argued, chemical compounds have identities that depend on their atomic and/or molecular structures, and not on their dispositions to behaviour, then what, if anything, follows about the status of the laws of behaviour of such structures? Does it, for example, follow that the laws of chemical behaviour are contingent? The argument that it does is this: If (1) the essences of molecular kinds are their atomic structures, and (2) atomic structures are categorical properties, then (3) chemical compounds can have no causal powers essentially, and the laws of chemical behaviour must be contingent. They cannot, as I argued in *Scientific Essentialism*, be metaphysically necessary.

However, it is not my contention that atomic structures are categorical properties. Certainly, I think that the identities of chemical compounds depend on their atomic structures, and the identities of these atomic structures depend on how the atomic parts are categorically and causally related to one another. But the whole message of scientific essentialism is that causal power derives from within. It is not imposed on things at any level of existence by laws of nature, or by anything else that might be conceived to be external to them. The flaw in the argument lies in its second premise. Atomic structures are not categorical properties, for the simple reason that the existence of

THE METAPHYSICS OF SCIENTIFIC REALISM

a structure implies the existence of the causally connected elements of that structure. And there is no reason to suppose that the elements of any atomic structure are lacking in causal powers. Nor is there any reason to think that the structure is just a spatial arrangement of these elements. There is presumably some kind of spatial arrangement of these elements in any given atomic structure. But that is not all there is. The parts must be causally bound to each other in various ways. So my answer to those who would suggest that the causal powers of molecules cannot be derived from their atomic structures is to ask: why not? There are plenty of causal powers embedded in molecular structures, and there is no reason whatever to suppose that the laws of behaviour of these structures are contingent.

Of course, I have no objection to saying that the laws concerning these things are *a posteriori*. But *a posteriority* does not imply contingency. It is true that nothing about behaviour follows just from a knowledge of the ways in which the atomic constituents of molecules are spatiotemporally arranged. For spatiotemporal arrangement is not a causal power. To deduce anything about their behaviour, we should need to know what the causal powers of the various atomic constituents are, where they are located within the categorical structure, and how they are disposed to respond to various kinds of physical or chemical stimuli when so located. For example, one cannot deduce that sugar will be soluble in water just from a knowledge of the distances between the atoms of water and sugar molecules. To draw any such conclusion, we should also need to have a really good theory of solubility, which is sufficient to explain how the sugar molecules, structured as they are, are disposed to react to the mass of water molecules.

A good theory of this kind would have to be able to tell us precisely what must be involved in any process of solution, if there is indeed only one such natural kind of process. Or, if there be more than one, then it would have to describe each of the natural kinds of processes that lead to the phenomenon of solution, and specify the necessary conditions for the relation of solvent to solute to hold for each such kind. To simplify the argument, let us assume that there is just one natural kind of process of solution. Then we should be able to state unequivocally what must exist if anything of kind A is to dissolve in anything of the kind B. And, plausibly, this is something that we might know if we knew enough about the causal powers of the atomic or subatomic parts of the atoms of A and B, and how they are arranged and disposed to interact with one another. Therefore, the solubility of sugar in water could still be a matter of metaphysical necessity. And in my view it is. Substances constituted in the sugar kind of way out of carbon, hydrogen and oxygen are intrinsically disposed to dissolve in substances constituted in the water kind of way out of hydrogen and oxygen. And, if this is true, then the proposition that sugar is soluble in water is metaphysically necessary.

There is, however, one consequence of this analysis: that a property that a thing of a given natural kind has necessarily may not, in fact, be an essential property of things of that kind. For the essential properties of a kind are those properties or structures in virtue of which a thing is a thing of this kind, and displays the manifest properties it does. In *Scientific Essentialism* I said:

> It is not just any old set of identifying properties, that is properties that are severally necessary and jointly sufficient for membership of the kind. The essential properties of a kind include all of the intrinsic properties and structures that together make a thing the kind of thing it is. (2001: 54–5)

But this was not quite right, nor, I think, quite what I meant. What I should have said is that the essential properties of a kind include all *and only* those intrinsic properties and structures that together make it the kind of thing it is. For my concept of real essence was clearly derived from Locke's. Sugar may (let us suppose) be identified by its solubility in water and sweetness of taste. But neither are essential properties of sugar. Neither is an intrinsic property of sugar, since neither is a property of sugar alone. For the same reason, it is not an essential property of water that it is capable of dissolving sugar. I suppose it to be a necessary truth that water has the capacity to dissolve sugar. But the composition and structure of water alone do not entail that it has this capacity. The existence of water does not even entail the existence of sugar. In a world without carbon atoms, indeed, there would be no sugar. However, the solubility of sugar in water is presumably a property that is necessarily displayed in all sugar-in-water systems. For the solubility of sugar in water is presumably derivable from the essential natures of these two substances. So, no doubt, it is also derivable from the essential nature of sugar that if there were any substance with the essential nature of water then sugar would be soluble in it. But it seems to me that the claim that sugar is soluble in water would be true only if both substances existed. So, I want to say that the essence of sugar is just its molecular structure. Its dispositions to behave, I would suppose, all derive from this, including its capacity to dissolve in any liquid substances with the molecular structure of water, if they should exist.

One could argue that the identities of the atoms included in any molecular structure may themselves depend not on their dispositions to behaviour, but on their subatomic constitutions, and so go on pushing the effective causal powers of things down to lower and lower levels. But if there are any truly elementary kinds of particles of substances in nature, then this process must have a natural limit. At some stage one will have to admit that the basic constituents of the world must behave as they do, because it is of their natures to do so. That is, the basic tenet of dispositional essentialism must be upheld.

6

REALISM AS FIRST PHILOSOPHY

The general theory of what exists most fundamentally is sometimes known as "first philosophy". The ontology of scientific realism could plausibly be developed to have such a role. As a first philosophy, it would have important implications for most kinds of enquiries. But the ontology of scientific realism, despite its name, may have less relevance to science itself than to other areas. For the metaphysics has been developed out of science, specifically to accommodate the developments that have occurred in this area. Practising scientists are unlikely to be familiar with many of the concepts employed in developing this ontology. Nevertheless, it is one that any scientific realist should be able to accept, and it makes good sense of the nature and structure of scientific knowledge: better, I claim, than any other ontology that has been developed so far. The theory is, perhaps, more likely to be influential in fields that have not been used as a basis for its development: in mathematics, for example, or in moral and political philosophy. For these areas, too, have their ontological presuppositions, and some of them are apparently contrary to the tenets of scientific realism. In this chapter, we shall examine some of these presuppositions, and consider how studies in these areas might be accommodated within a scientific realist metaphysical framework.

Realism in mathematics

As a philosopher of science I was always taught to believe that mathematics was essentially different from any of the sciences. Its truths were necessary, and therefore not in need of truthmakers. If they were not logically necessary, as the propositions of logic were supposed to be, then they were true by definition or convention, or were the logical consequences of such propositions. Therefore, the propositions of mathematics were not thought to be true in the same sense as the truths of empirical science. The correspondence theory of truth was not supposed to be relevant to mathematics, according to most philosophers I knew. Mathematical truth had somehow to be an internalist concept. Consequently, much of the debate in the philosophy of mathematics was about how mathematical truth was to be defined. Was it to be equated to provability? But, if so, what sense could one then make of Kurt Gödel's theorem to the effect that if arithmetic is consistent, then there are propositions of arithmetic that are true but unprovable. There were, therefore, doubts about the applicability of the law of the excluded middle in mathematics. Could Gödel's beautiful proof of the essential incompleteness of any consistent axiomatization of arithmetic really be accepted at face value?

I really do not have anything new to add to the details of any of these debates about mathematical truth. But it may be worthwhile to point out that scientific essentialism has changed the ground rules for them. It does so by denying the common premise that what is necessarily true must be either formally true, as logic is, or true by definition or convention, or a logical consequence of propositions that are true by definition or convention. Scientific essentialism challenges this, because it postulates the existence of metaphysical necessities. And, metaphysical necessity is different from any form of necessity I had ever heard of as a student. A metaphysically necessary proposition is one that is true in virtue of the essential natures of things. And these essential natures of things are, in general, discoverable empirically. For they are the intrinsic properties or structures of the members of natural kinds in virtue of which they are things of these kinds. Water, for example, is essentially H_2O. But this is neither a logical truth, nor a proposition that is true by definition (unless one means "real definition", which is different), nor a logical consequence of any such definitions.

Therefore, if there are any mathematical truths that are meta-physically necessary, there is indeed the possibility that these truths have truthmakers, in the way, for example, that the laws of nature have truthmakers. Scientific essentialism thus creates an opening for mathematical realism, since a realist in mathematics is simply one who believes that many of the basic truths of mathematics are both necessary and grounded in reality.

The idea that I wish to explore is that mathematics is the formal study of the categorical dimensions of things (as I have defined them in Chapter 5). Consider first the concept of number. Number is, fundamentally, a dimension of natural or stipulated classes of things, since it is a respect in which such classes of things may objectively be the same or different. There are plenty of natural classes of things to which we can appeal to give this concept of number as a dimension some bite. We may, for example, consider the classes of fingers on our hands, petals on a flower, corners of a triangle or magnetic polarities, and enquire whether any of these natural classes of things happen to be the same or different in number. But there is no need to limit the dimension of number to such more or less natural classes. For stipulated classes of things also have the property of number, and the values of this property may easily be compared with the actual values of the property of number displayed by natural classes. Remember that the values of the property of number are all of the possible infimic species of this property.

Let us call the values of this natural property of number "the natural numbers", and consider the class of all natural numbers. This class is necessarily an infinite one. For one can always add another thing by stipulation to any possible class, thus creating a class whose number is one greater than the class from which it was constructed. Moreover, the class of all natural numbers is necessarily a class of real things. For the natural numbers correspond to all of the real possibilities of constructing classes of things out of existing classes by adding one more thing. So, my answer to the question "Do the natural numbers exist?" is yes. For the natural numbers are just the values of the natural dimension of number: those values that are constructible from a unitary base by the process of adding one more thing. The natural dimension of number certainly exists; it is one of the basic categorical dimensions of nature. The process of adding one to a given class by stipulation is a real process, which anyone could carry out, and the possibilities of construction are real possibilities. Therefore, the natural numbers are real, even though they may not all be actual.

Consider next the dimension of spatial location. The set of all values of this dimension is the set of all possible spatial locations. To define a location in a Newtonian three-dimensional world, it would be sufficient to give its spatial coordinates in a coordinate frame that is at rest relative to absolute space. And the sets of all such coordinates for a given frame would then define the set of all possible locations in that space. However, we now know that the actual world is not such a world. We have a fairly clear concept of what it is for two events to occur at the same place locally. But we have no clear concept of what it is for two events to occur at the same place absolutely. So the dimension of location has to be relativized somehow, if we are to capture mathematically some more generally applicable concepts of sameness and difference in place. Hermann Minkowski showed us how to construct the relevant geometry for a world of the kind described in Einstein's special theory of relativity. Is the real world, then, such a world? No, I do not think so. But there is a real question of the shape of space or space–time, and mathematicians may eventually help us to answer this question.

Realism in the philosophy of mathematics, wherever it has existed, has nearly always been strongly influenced by Platonism, and therefore by a philosophy that is antithetical to theories of properties and relations that are of Aristotelian origin. But one advantage of thinking of mathematics as the formal study of the categorical dimensions of nature is that is allows us to regard mathematical entities simply as the values of properties: properties that are instantiated as all Aristotelian properties must be, but ones that may also have values that are not actual values. Science has a long tradition of using variables that do not range only over actual values to describe the causal processes of nature. I think that mathematicians should be allowed to do the same, in constructing their theories of the categorical dimensions.

I am aware that these remarks on mathematical realism will be considered to be far too cursory to be worth much. But the task of developing a realist philosophy of mathematics along these lines would be immense, and probably beyond me. However, Bigelow (1988) has made a good start on a related project in his book *The Reality of Numbers*, and I am encouraged by his work to think that it can be carried through successfully. My only contribution to it, at this stage, is to suggest that the concept of a categorical dimension may prove to be one we most need to work with, if our aim is to develop a realist philosophy of mathematics. For, given the concept of a categorical dimension, we can easily define many, if not all, of the required Platonic universals that are needed, and, plausibly, a great deal of mathematics can be seen as consisting of abstract theories concerning the ranges of the dimensions of which these universals are values. The evident Platonism of much mathematics is thus no barrier to our offering a realistic account of it. The categorical dimensions of the world, which I would suppose to be the true subject matter of mathematics, are not fictional, or even Platonic ideals. They are among the most basic properties in nature; and, naturally, the more general the dimensions are, the more fundamental they are, and the more fundamental the theory of them would be.

Realism about time

Realists about time believe that time is essentially concerned with the rates of change occurring in various kinds of natural processes. Therefore, if, as a realist, one believes that there is such a thing as global time, one must also believe that there is a process of global evolution to which it refers. Moreover, one must also believe that the topology of time must derive from the nature of this global process. Therefore, if the world's process has a beginning or an end, then time must have a beginning or an end; if it is circular, then time must be circular; and so on. But most philosophers concerned with time are not realists in this sense. Most of them think of the universe as a four-dimensional block structure in which time is a fourth dimension that is orthogonal to the three spatial ones, and would reject all talk of global evolution as muddleheaded. But, in the view that is to be urged here, most philosophers are wrong about this. They have been too influenced by early-twentieth-century positivism. Despite their arguments to the contrary, there is an objective distinction between past and future, and a physical mechanism located in the past that generates the future. The so-called "passage" of time, which is generated by this process, is a real phenomenon.

According to quantum mechanical realism, elementary causal processes are physical systems. For they are temporally extended and intrinsically conservative of all of the conserved quantities. The same is presumably true of all physical causal processes, including those that, according to the ontology of physical realism developed in Chapter 5, constitute physical objects. These elementary causal processes all have one very striking property: they culminate in events of particle realization, producing determinate physical states that had not existed until then. So, if these processes are the elements of physical causal processes generally, then all such processes must be the generators of new determinate states of reality. Causality was once described as the "cement of the universe", a metaphor that suggests that causes and their effects are necessarily coexisting in an overall spatiotemporal structure. But if the elementary causal processes of the world involve quantum mechanically indeterministic energy transfer processes that are brought to an end by absorption events, they would, perhaps, be better described as the generators of their effects. But, if this is so, then it has profound consequences for the theory of time.

"Presentist" and "growing block" theorists about time have generally spoken of a process of "becoming", or perhaps more usually of "temporal passage". In both cases, the future is conceived as being something that exists, becomes the present and eventually becomes the past. But, according to quantum mechanical realism, the process is likely to be one of generation rather than of becoming or passing. For there is a natural physical interpretation of the process of generating the future, namely, that of particle realization. This process is clearly involved in the causal realization of new determinate states of reality, including new "time slices" of existing objects, or new effects of past events, such as observations of events on other galaxies, or observations of the background radiation that was supposedly emitted at the time of the Big Bang. So, I prefer to speak of "temporal generation", rather than temporal passage. For the process of temporal generation is plausibly nothing other than that of generating new determinate states of affairs, just like the states of affairs that we know exist today, and have existed in the past.

The process of particle realization is one that exists independently of human consciousness, and is not specifically related to human observation. Nevertheless, its identification as the process of temporal generation would undoubtedly explain why the world appears to us to be evolving as it does. For, according to quantum mechanical realism, every new occurrence of this process would result in a new determinate event. And events of this kind are presumably going on in our heads, just as we speak. The theory thus allows us, in keeping with the realist stance, to say that the world appears to be evolving as it does, because in fact it is evolving in this way (or, in the case of galactic changes, because it was evolving as it now appears to be). Therefore, the process of particle realization would seem to be a good candidate for the role of generator of the future, if such a role were thought to be required. Certainly, it is much better than McCall's process of branch attrition, because what is required for the role of generator of the future is not an external process of the sort he postulates, but an internal one: one that is intrinsically grounded in the things that produced all of the Schrödinger waves that have not yet been realized.

But do we have to go this way? Do we need a mechanism for generating the future? Block universe theorists (four-dimensionalists) will naturally deny that we do. But, at the same time, they must accept the challenge of explaining the illusion of temporal passage, and justify their contention that future and past events all have the same status. This is itself a difficult problem. But there is much more that is required if four-dimensionalism is to be defended. For, as Price has argued, four-dimensionalists should also be committed to the T-reversibility thesis, and hence to the view that the directedness of time (from past to future) is an illusion, or at least an artefact of the conditions that existed in the distant past. So far, none of these issues have been satisfactorily resolved.

But, against this, it may be argued that four-dimensionalism has much to offer: the theories of special and general relativity are at least as powerful and empirically well established as any of those of quantum mechanics. So, the ontology required for science must be adequate for these theories too. Four-dimensionalism, it is said, is the preferred spatiotemporal framework for the theories in question, and so its role as such a framework must be preserved in any new ontology. This point is well taken, and I do not wish to challenge it. In any case, it is not necessary to do so, because the special and general theories of relativity are really theories about the shape and limits of energy transfer processes, and it is entirely reasonable that we should abstract from the temporal directedness of time in the construction of such theories. For the known laws of energy transfer (including Schrödinger's equation) are all T-symmetric, and do not require a knowledge of temporal direction. The only conception of time that is strictly required for the theory of these laws is just one of temporal interval: one that is formally analogous to that of spatial interval. Therefore, if our aim is only to develop a general theory of energy transfer processes, adequate for all possible processes of this kind, we do not need the more complete conception of time that is required for quantum mechanics. The limited conception of time as space-like, that is, as temporal interval, is all we need. The four-dimensionalist framework that is required for the theories of relativity may therefore be retained, even if a much richer conception of time is ultimately required for quantum mechanical realism, and for ontology.

It may also be argued that temporal generation is not objectively definable. For, to define it, it seems that we must be able to say what it is for past events to generate present or future ones. But to do so objectively, we surely must have objective concepts of past, present or future. They need not be objectively determinable concepts, since we are not arguing here within a positivistic or conventionalist framework. Even so, it is not clear that any of these concepts is objectively definable, even metaphysically. Is there, for example, a past that is metaphysically different from the future? If so, then the present could perhaps be defined as the frontier between these two regions. Or, is there always a time that we could objectively identify as "the present"? If so, then we could perhaps identify the future as that which is future relative to this objective present, and the past as that which was past relative to it.

Let us begin with the concept of the present. We know that our utterances have locations in time, just as our bodies have positions in space, and that these concepts can be defined satisfactorily, or sharpened up appropriately, for the purposes of physical theory. But "the present" does not seem to be definable at all, except in a token-reflexive way. If it is defined as the time at which I am now speaking, then this gets us nowhere beyond our present experience. For "now" is a term that requires a human perspective: to understand its reference, we need to know the context of its utterance. This problem could be solved if an objective distinction could be made between two mutually exclusive classes of times, ones that we could identify as "the past" and "the future". For then we should be able to define "the present" simply as the border between them. But, so far, no one has been able to make such a distinction. The past is what is past relative to a given speaker at a given time, and the corresponding future is what is future relative to that speaker. But for workable scientific concepts of past, present or future, we need ones that are not speaker-relative.

A metaphysical hypothesis has to meet two requirements: it must be consistent with the known facts, and be part of a unifying account of reality that explains the overall structure of what we are able to observe. Given quantum mechanical realism, the following conditions must all be satisfied: (a) the future, from any given temporal perspective, has no fixed or metaphysically determinate events, and so is essentially, and hence ontologically, different from the past from that perspective; (b) there is a quantum mechanical mechanism, namely, particle realization, that would explain the generation of past determinate states of being from the determinate states that pre-existed them; and (c) there is good reason to suppose that this mechanism is still operating. My hypothesis F is this: *The future is the same from every place that is at rest relative to the rest of the universe; it is not just the future relative to us as observers in the Milky Way: it is the same for everyone.* It is a future that is constantly being generated by physical processes of the kinds described by quantum mechanics, some of which were presumably begun at the time of the Big Bang. This hypothesis is certainly consistent with the view that the future is generated by the events that are occurring now, or have occurred in the past. Moreover, it explains why the future appears to us to be essentially different from the past, and why we all have what four-dimensionalists normally regard as a "persistent illusion" of time passing. It explains it, because, given a physicalist theory of mind, our self-awareness is in fact our present consciousness of our own brain processes, including presumably some of the physical causal processes that are now occurring in our heads.

The objective present

It is widely accepted that the existence of a physical causal order for time is sufficient for the purposes of relativity theory. For it enables us to distinguish objectively between the local present, its absolute past and its absolute future. The absolute past of any event is represented by the region in the downward light-cone of a standard space–time diagram, where this event is supposedly located at the origin. The absolute future of this event is then represented by the region within the upward light-cone. The region outside this double light-cone is called the topological present. According to special relativity theory, there must always be an inertial frame of reference with respect to which any point within the topological present is in standard signal synchrony with the locally present event. Events occurring within this region are also said to have a space-like separation from those occurring at the origin. For again, according to special relativity theory, neither can be the cause nor the effect of the other. Events involving the collapses of wavefronts, and other non-local phenomena, are topologically simultaneous with each other. So, there must be reference frames with respect to which these phenomena are in standard signal synchrony. Presumably, they are the frames of reference defined by the wavefronts of the collapsing Schrödinger waves in the one kind of case, and that of the apparatus in the case of the spin determinations of entangled particles.

Given that the theories of special and general relativity are the theories of the energy transfer processes required for macro-mechanics and electromagnetism, the theory of space–time required for these theories need not be complete. Indeed, we have seen that there is good reason to believe that it is incomplete. For, while topological simultaneity may be all that is needed for special relativity, it is evidently not all that is needed for quantum mechanics. The instantaneous collapses of wavefronts described in quantum mechanics would seem to need a much sharper definition of simultaneity.

Nor is it obvious that topological simultaneity is sufficient for cosmology. On the contrary, cosmologists have a concept of objective simultaneity, which they take to mean something like "temporally equidistant from the Big Bang". From their point of view, it is obvious that looking at the world from a spaceship moving at a speed close to that of light would give one a very distorted view of reality. To such an observer travelling in the direction of Andromeda, for example, Andromeda itself, and all of the galaxies beyond Andromeda, would be strongly blue-shifted, while light from all of the galaxies behind the spaceship would be strongly red-shifted. So, the occupants of the spaceship would know that they were moving fast with respect to the rest of the universe, in which direction they were moving and roughly how fast they were moving. From the point of view of observers on earth, the light from galaxies that are more or less equidistant from the Milky Way is red-shifted to roughly the same degree, and the magnitude of the red-shift increases more or less uniformly with distance. Presumably this is true from every vantage point in the universe that is relatively more or less stationary with respect to the rest of the universe. Therefore, it is not true in general that there is an equivalence of the reference frames that might be used to define simultaneities over vast distances. Rapidly moving frames (relative to earth) cannot sensibly be regarded as equivalent to stationary ones. The only ones that are reasonably acceptable for determining simultaneity relationships over vast astronomical distances are those that are moving only quite slowly relative to earth: slowly enough for the fact of motion not to distort the wavelengths of the light waves received from different directions in space.

My hypothesis F is compatible with these facts, and is indeed the generally accepted view of cosmologists. For cosmologists have to make precisely this assumption when they are calculating the value of the Hubble constant H_0 in the equation

$$v = H_0 D$$

where v is the recessional velocity of any given galaxy, H_0 is the value of H in Friedmann's equations taken at the time of observation, and D is the "co-moving proper distance"[1] from the galaxy to the observer in the three-dimensional space defined by cosmological time, that is, by time since the Big Bang. (Note that the time interval from the Big Bang to the local present here is taken to be the same as the time interval from the Big Bang to the local present anywhere else in the universe.

---

1. This phrase is taken from the Wikipedia article on Hubble's law.

Therefore, if this cosmological point of view is accepted, it follows that the local present is not just a local present: it is a global one.)

Cosmological time T (or Hubble time, as it is sometimes called) may be defined as $1/H$, where H is the parameter whose present value is H_0. According to modern cosmology, this common time is objective, that is, the same for observers everywhere. Therefore, there is no need to specify a reference frame for the measurement of cosmological time. Any reference frame that is more or less stationary with respect to the bulk of the universe will do for the purposes of measurement. In my view, the frame should be considered to be that of the initial radiation from the Big Bang. For, if the process of photon realization is truly instantaneous, as I am supposing, then every such event is a global one, including all those that are occurring now.

The rate of expansion of the universe

Given that there is an objective present, it follows that cosmological time, which measures the age of the universe, must be an objective quantity. So the question naturally arises: how does cosmological time compare with local time? The answer is that the two must be the same now, since, by definition, every sound measure of the local time-interval in any normal frame of reference is necessarily a sound measure of the global time-interval. But the two are not conceptually the same. For all that we know, the rate of recession of the galaxies could be speeding up or slowing down compared with the internal processes of rotation, vibration, radioactive decay and so on that are used to measure local time. If $d^2T/dt^2 = 0$, then we are in a steady state universe. But this may not be the way the world is. The universe might be expanding ever more rapidly, or it might be decelerating. The Hubble expansion is usually explained by assuming that the galaxies are all located on the three-dimensional surface of an expanding four-dimensional sphere. The fourth dimension that is supposed to drive the expansion is thought to be the cosmological time T. But in my view, cosmological time does not do anything at all. The physical causal processes set in train by the Big Bang are presumably the ones that are driving the expansion of the universe. Therefore, the interesting question is whether d^2T/dt^2 is greater than, equal to or less than zero. For this will answer the question of whether the energy transmission processes of nature are speeding up, keeping pace with or slowing down relative to other natural kinds of processes, for example those of radioactive decay. If they are speeding up, then this would be some reason to think that the rate of expansion of the universe is increasing. If they are slowing down, then we might surmise that the rate of expansion of the universe is slowing down. In my view, the value of dT/dt, which is the rate of temporal generation (or "temporal passage", if you have a different metaphysics from me) must be geared to the velocity of light. For the global wavefront that collapses when a light signal from the Big Bang is observed is what most plausibly defines the frontier between past and future. If the velocity of light has been constant since the Big Bang, then $d^2T/dt^2 = 0$. Otherwise, it must be a function of T with the current value of 1.

Generating the future

The emission and absorption events occurring in the objective past are localized, and in this and other ways they are metaphysically determinate. They have physical properties and are physically related to one another. They are dotted about almost everywhere in the past. However, they do not occur at random. For there are chains of closely packed dots, which we should all recognize as space–time worms, and other space–time structures reflecting larger-scale patterns of behaviour. Each past absorption event is linked by a Schrödinger wave to a past emission in the lower light cone of that absorption event. In the case of a space–time worm, these past emissions are mainly from localized events occurring in its earlier stages. But not every past energy emission is linked to a past energy absorption. For there must be some Schrödinger waves that are "still in progress", that is, have not yet resulted in particle realizations. There are, therefore, various metaphysical truths about the past, that is, propositions that have truthmakers.[2]

---

2. By a "truthmaker for p", I mean an existent whose existence metaphysically necessitates p.

The future, on the other hand, has no such determinate events, and hence the space–time worms of things do not extend into the future. They are not unconnected with the future; for most of the things that now exist will continue to do so, and thus grow into the future. But propositions about the future are not made true by anything that exists now or ever has existed. They might perhaps be made certain or highly probable by things that will exist. But they are not now true in this sense. Their status is essentially different from that of propositions about the past. For the events of the past are determinate all the way back to the Big Bang. In saying this, I do not mean that they are *epistemically* determinate. I mean only that there is a fact of the matter about them. But there is no fact of the matter concerning propositions about the future. There are grounds for believing things about the future, indeed conclusive grounds for doing so. But the present or past states of affairs that are the truthmakers for these grounds are not the truthmakers for any propositions about the future. They are just grounds for believing that certain of our reasonable expectations will be realized.

There are timeless sorts of truths that have implications for the future, for example the laws of nature. But, as I have argued elsewhere, these propositions are metaphysically necessary, and so have timeless truthmakers such as essential properties, causal powers or natural kind memberships. They will, no doubt, be confirmed by what will happen, just as they have been confirmed by what has happened. But they are not made true by anything that has happened or will happen. They are made true only by things existing and being constituted by the natural kinds of things they are, and by the ways in which things of these kinds are naturally disposed to behave.

The future is therefore very different from the past, and the process of temporal generation is one that literally changes the world. The process that brings this about is plausibly the familiar quantum mechanical process of particle realization, and, as such, it is one that is internally driven. It is not a mysterious process of becoming that somehow reveals what already exists. Nor is it one of passage into a future world, as the psychologizers of time would have us believe. It is one of generation from what already exists by the energy transfer processes of nature, and the particle realizations they produce.

Realism and human freedom

The consequences of the ontology that is being developed here for our moral and political theories of freedom, rights, obligations and responsibilities are as dramatic as they are for time. For, as we shall see, all of these concepts must be revised in the light of the new realist ontology. The key concept for both moral and political theories is that of human freedom. For, if we change this to a scientifically more realistic one, we must change all of the other basic concepts of morality. If we still thought, as Descartes did, that the substance of our minds was essentially different from that of our bodies, then we should be likely to have a very different view about ourselves, and about the society we have created, than we would have if we accepted an ontology of scientific realism. We should, for example, be likely to think of ourselves as embodied spirits, capable of thinking, reasoning and deciding things independently of any physical processes that might be going on in our heads. We might even think that such a conception of human beings is required if we are ever to accept moral responsibility for what we do. Consequently, some people might well be wary of the philosophy of scientific realism that is being developed here, and see it as a threat to the moral order. Some religious people are likely to feel much the same way, but for a different reason. Religiously authorized moral precepts are commonly regarded as the commands of God. Consequently, many religious people would say that all morality is ultimately sourced in God, and that to accept the ontology of scientific realism would be to leave no place for morality in human affairs.

In what remains of this chapter, it will be argued that the concept of human freedom that is generally presupposed in moral and political theory will have to be revised if the ontology of scientific realism is to be accepted as our first philosophy. The idea that human beings are unique among animal species in being the possessors of a special kind of rationally determined agency that would allow them to act independently of the causal order of the universe would clearly have to be rejected. For human beings must be bound by causal laws just as much as any other organism, and the whole idea that we could somehow step around this restriction cannot be accepted together with an overarching philosophy of scientific realism. Nor does the indeterminacy of causality, discussed in Chapter 4, make the case for a special kind of rationally determined agency any easier to make. For the idea that human beings, alone in all creation, could act with rational determinism in an indeterministic world of the kind described by quantum mechanics could not possibly be anything more than wishful thinking. We are bound to act as we are caused to act, just as much as any other creature, even though it may well be true that our behaviour is less predictable than the behaviour of other animals. If our behaviour is in fact less predictable, this would be mainly because more of the causing is going on inside our heads, not because more of it is being caused physically.

Philosophers have been well aware of this for some time, and most philosophers would either defend some form of compatibilism between scientific realism and free will, or else argue that free will does not exist. In what follows I shall argue for a form of compatibilism, rather than the nihilistic alternative that free will does not exist. That is, I shall argue for a conception of freedom of the will that is compatible with scientific realism. And, if this should prove to be incompatible with accepted moral theories, then so much the worse for these theories. In what follows, it will be argued that the concept of free will as rationally determined agency that has occupied centre stage in moral philosophy since the seventeenth century has to be rejected.

Rejection of this classical idea of human freedom has many important consequences. First, it allows us to recognize that there are significant moral agents other than individuals in most societies. For, if we adopt a compatibilist theory of moral responsibility, there is no good reason why the major contributors to the well-being or otherwise of people – governments, churches, corporations, universities, hospitals, armies, police forces and schools, among others – should not all be considered to be moral agents. And this is certainly desirable. For these various organizations are undoubtedly among the most powerful forces for good or ill in all modern societies. But, in fact, they are seldom regarded as having that special kind of freedom of choice required for moral agency. Consequently, the moral regulation of such organizations has always had to be indirect, and is, consequently, usually ineffective. Chief executive officers have to be told not to be greedy, or to show due concern for the well-being of their customers or workforces. But they can just nod their heads, and do what they would have done anyway. For individuals are rarely seen as being wholly in charge of the organizations they are said to be responsible for, and individual responsibility for one's bit-role in group decisions is notoriously hard to pin down. Secondly, a compatibilist conception of freedom of choice should also allow us to say that individuals have moral responsibilities that depend on their social roles, as well as those that depend only on their natures as human beings. But currently, the moral regulation of professionals, and other specialists in society, has to be achieved indirectly, for example, through a supposed duty of care applicable to all individuals that happen to be performing a service.

On the other hand, if we were to adopt a theory of freedom of choice compatible with a realist ontology, we may be forced to adopt correlative theories of moral responsibilities, rights and obligations. For these theories are all interrelated. But this may, or may not, be a bad thing. There are no generally accepted theories of moral rights, obligations or responsibilities based on libertarian or religious theories of freedom of choice, and it may prove to be advantageous to make a fresh approach to these issues. In the following sections, I shall outline a theory of human freedom that any scientific realist should be able to accept and, in Chapter 7, explore the consequences of accepting it as a basis of a theory of moral responsibility. I shall then proceed to develop correlative theories of moral rights and obligations.

Freedom of choice

The problem of free choice is not whether it exists, but what it is. We know it exists because we are all conscious of the processes of deliberation involved in decision-making, and of being able to act on the decisions we have made. These processes are presumably not just charades. At least, from the point of view of a scientific realist, the onus of proof must be on those who would suppose that they are. So, for a scientific realist, the important questions must be: (a) what are these processes; and (b) what ends do they serve? Briefly, my answers are: (a) the processes are deliberative ones that are capable of changing, modifying or reinforcing the current behavioural dispositions of the agent making the choice; and (b) their point is to ensure that whatever actions the agent may eventually take, when he/she/it is act-ing freely regarding the matter under consideration, they will prove to be ones that are acceptable to the agent, given the agent's current preferences.

The usual assumption is that an act of free choice must involve an act of will. And an act of will is normally supposed to be a delibera-tive act that determines a course of action that, until that moment, was undetermined. Thus free will is conceived to be a power to inter-vene in the course of nature: specifically, to make appropriate choices and implement them. But if this assumption were correct, then the scientific worldview, which we are presupposing here, would have to be false. For in an essentially indeterministic world such as ours, there is no possible mechanism for choosing from the range of possi-bilities that are still theoretically open. And, in a world that is causally as determinate as ours at the macroscopic level, there is no room for choice. Therefore, according to the scientific worldview, there is no, and cannot be, any human power of the kind required to intervene in the course of nature. Therefore, free will, as classically conceived by libertarians, is incompatible with the scientific worldview.

Nevertheless, we can, and often do, choose freely. Therefore, choosing freely to act in one way rather then another, and acting on this decision, does not, indeed could not possibly, involve any classically conceived act of will. And, since this is so, human beings may not be the only agents that are capable of choosing freely to act in one way rather than another, or acting on their own decisions. Various collective agents whose management teams deliberate about what courses of action to take in the circumstances they face may be no less capable of exercising freedom of choice than individuals. Corporations are expected to bear the interests of shareholders in mind, hospitals to have regard for the interests of their patients, uni-versities to be concerned with the quality of student education, and so on. But when a vote is taken on what to do, the fact that several individual agents have to make up their minds about the issue, and vote accordingly, does not make the decision that is made any more or less free than if the decision had been made by one person alone. If the collective decision-making process is one of the required delib-erative kind, and it establishes a disposition of the collective agent to act, as and when the occasion demands, in a way that will, overall, be acceptable to the collective agent, then there is no reason why this decision should not be considered to be an act of free will.

The taking of a decision by an individual or collective agent on a proposed course of action is an event that establishes or reinforces a disposition of the agent to act in some particular way: normally, when the time for action on the matter is judged to be right. There is nothing supernatural about this, nothing that requires an extraordinary mechanism of the kind that traditional free will theory postulates. All that is required for this to occur is that the agent should, by a process of deliberation, be able to acquire some new disposition that could, in principle, be triggered by the act of judging by the agent, or by the agent's appointed agent, that the present time is apt for the proposed course of action. Such judgements can be made by individual agents, made collectively, or made by individuals in the relevant organizations whose jobs are to carry out management's decisions.

Nor is there anything extraordinary in an individual or collective agent being able to acquire new dispositions to act. Higher animals do it all the time. It is called "learning by experience". Human beings may be unusual in having the capacity to learn from remembered or recorded experience. But the step from animal to human learning capacities is not so great as to be inexplicable biologically. Therefore, it is not contrary to the scientific image of the world to suppose that human beings have this rather special capacity. We do not have to suppose, as some libertarians do, that we are God-like creatures able to act with deliberative determination independently of the forces of nature to explain this unusual capacity. The capacity to learn from past experience by reflection on it is just a natural extension of the powers enjoyed by every intelligent creature. And if we can exercise this power, so can every organization that depends on this ability of ours. And, if we can be said to be morally responsible for our freely made choices just because of it, so can every collective agent that has the same power to make such choices.

Human agency

If one is a scientific realist, then one should be a realist about causal powers. That is, one should accept them as being what they purport to be, namely, capacities to make certain things happen as a matter of course, when the appropriate conditions for triggering them are realized. But, perhaps surprisingly, not every scientific realist does accept this obvious conclusion. Scientific realists normally pride themselves on their hard-headed realism about theoretical entities in science, and are strongly resistant to most reductionist tendencies. Causal powers are prominent among the theoretical entities postulated in science, and there are no good reasons for being realists about things like electrons and positrons that are not also good reasons for being realists about their causal powers. Yet, such is the influence of Hume in the theory of causation that many scientific realists have followed his lead by accepting regularity theories of causal influence.

However, the philosophical tide has now turned against Hume on causation, and there is widespread agreement that his regularity theory is inadequate.[3] We are all consciously aware of our decisions to do things being followed by actions performed to carry them out. So, those who accept Hume's theory would have no difficulty in thinking of our decisions as being the causes of our actions. Moreover, we are all consciously aware of our deliberations being the forerunners of our decisions. So, regularity theorists would naturally be inclined to think that our deliberations are the causes of our decisions. But if our deliberations are the causes of our decisions, our responsibility for our decisions must depend on our responsibility for our deliberations. But then the question arises of how or why we are morally responsible for our deliberations. What is our role as an agent? We do not often deliberate

---

3. See R. Harré & E. H. Madden, *Causal Powers: A Theory of Natural Necessity* (Oxford: Blackwell, 1975); C. Swoyer, "The Nature of Natural Laws", *Australasian Journal of Philosophy* **60** (1982), 203–23; D. M. Armstrong, *What is a Law of Nature?* (Cambridge: Cambridge University Press, 1983); N. Cartwright, *Nature's Capacities and their Measurement* (Oxford: Oxford University Press, 1989); E. Fales, *Causation and Universals* (London: Routledge & Kegan Paul, 1990); C. B. Martin, "The Need for Ontology: Some Choices", *Philosophy* **68** (1993), 505–22 and "Powers for Realists", in *Ontology, Causality and Mind*, J. Bacon *et al.* (eds), 175–92 (Cambridge: Cambridge University Press, 1993); J. W. Carroll, *Laws of Nature* (Cambridge: Cambridge University Press, 1994); G. Molnar, *Powers: A Study in Metaphysics*, S. Mumford (ed.) (Oxford: Oxford University Press, 2003); Shoemaker, "Causality and Properties"; and my *Scientific Essentialism*.

on what we will consider to be relevant to the making of a given decision, or, if we do sometimes do so, it does not seem to make us any more or less responsible. Mental events occur in sequence, we seem obliged to say, but the idea that one has, or could have, any control over what one thinks or decides would appear to be untenable. So, Humeanism seems to be *prima facie* incompatible with human agency.

If one is a realist about causal powers, however, then the gap no longer seems to be so wide. For everything that has a causal power must be an agent of some kind. This is not to say, of course, that everything that has a causal power has autonomy, or is capable of exercising free choice. It does not. But there would appear to be at least the possibility of regarding human agents as a species of natural agents.

The analysis of human free choice that I wish to present rests on the concept of a meta-causal power, and the claim that meta-causal powers of a certain kind are deeply involved in the exercise of human agency. Meta-causal powers, like all other causal powers, are dispositional properties. However, there are many different kinds of dispositional properties, and not all of them are causal powers. To say that X is disposed to do Y in circumstances C is to say that X would do Y if the circumstances C were to be realized. But to say that X has the causal power to do Y in circumstances C is to say that X would be caused to do Y if the circumstances C were to be realized. But things can be disposed to do things of certain kinds if they are left to themselves. A body that is moving inertially, for example, has a disposition to continue to do so, and it will continue in just this way unless or until something interferes with it. The same with a photon: it will continue to be propagated in accordance with the laws of electromagnetic radiation unless or until it is absorbed. Let us call dispositional properties of these kinds "inertial powers", and reserve the term "causal powers" for those that have to be activated or "triggered" in some way, if they are to have any effect. But there are other kinds of dispositional properties too. Some are unconditional, such as the disposition of a radioactive nucleus (or other particle) to decay in one way or another. And for these unconditional dispositions there are just certain probabilities attaching to the various possible decay modes, but no triggering or inhibiting conditions. Such dispositional properties are usually called "propensities". The causal powers that are of primary concern in this chapter, however, are those that I am calling "meta-causal powers". They are powers that require to be triggered, as all strict causal powers do, but have new or altered causal powers among their effects.

The effects of the meta-causal powers that operate in the processes of autonomous decision-making are dispositions to act in certain sorts of ways if the agent were to judge the circumstances to be appropriate. The causal power that would thus be established must therefore be one that would be triggered, if at all, by the making of a judgement, namely, a judgement to the effect that the circumstances would now be appropriate to do whatever it was that one had in mind. It is true that most of the time, we rely on our established dispositions to guide our actions, and then act on them as and when we judge it appropriate to do so. And, most of the time, we are not conscious, or hardly conscious, of the judgements we have made about the appropriateness of the times or circumstances for our proposed actions. It is as if thinking of them is all that is required to realize them. But we know that it is not all that is required, because we are all able to contemplate an action without doing it, or put off doing what we have already decided to do to another time, or another place. Some philosophers have said that an act of willing is required if we are actually to do what we have already decided to do. But such an extraordinary explanation is neither required nor tenable.

A power of agency of the kind enjoyed by human beings appears to be fairly unique in the animal kingdom. If other animals have any freedom of choice, it must be much more limited than the freedom that we enjoy. For, to have this power, we not only need the capacity to engage in the reflective processes of rational decision-making, but must also have the power to act on any decisions that we might reach. We certainly have all of these capacities. But it is doubtful whether any other animal has either a developed capacity to engage in processes of learning by reflection on experience, or the degrees of knowledge, or of self-knowledge, that would be required to make the judgements necessary to trigger the acquired dispositions to act.

But one important question remains: how could we ever have initiated a process of learning retrospectively from experience in the first place? And what do we have to do to initiate such a process? We do it, I suggest, simply by recognizing that the issue we are concerned with is one that needs to be decided. That is, we make the judgement that a decision, or a review of previous decisions, is required to settle what is to be done. And this answer will suffice, provided that we already have a disposition to engage in rational decision-making in such circumstances. But this is not itself a disposition that we could have acquired rationally. For this would require that we needed the disposition in order to acquire it. My hypothesis is that human beings acquired the disposition to make choices by rational reflection, not by rationally considering the matter, but by the blind processes of natural selection. The capacities to learn retrospectively from experience, and act on the information so obtained, were selected because of their survival value.

Personal and collective responsibility

One philosopher who has tried with more success than most to articulate adequate concepts of freedom and agency is Philip Pettit (2001). In doing so, he focused on the phenomenology of responsible decision-making, and argued that to act as an agent, and thus to have moral responsibility for a given choice or action, one has to be, as he says, "in discursive control" of it, in the sorts of ways that agents normally are. This is correct, I believe. But human agents are not the only agents that are in discursive control of decision-making. Every academic board, house of parliament, board of directors, synod and meeting of army chiefs of staff is in discursive control of the issues they are discussing. Therefore, by Pettit's criteria, they are all agents that are morally responsible for their actions. I accept Pettit's criteria, and also this implication, which most moral theorists seem very reluctant to accept.

It is likely to be objected that Pettit's theory of freedom of the will does not do enough to justify our status as potentially autonomous agents who are capable of being morally responsible for our own choices and actions. If we have the meta-causal power to choose between alternative courses of action, and exercise this power on demand, as I am supposing, then there is a clear sense in which any considered choice we might eventually make must be our own. For, certainly, we will have initiated the process, decided the outcome on the basis of our own knowledge and past experience, and acted on it by judging that the circumstances are apt for doing so. So, in the case of individual human agents, let us agree that (a) they are *personally* responsible for the choices they make when they make them freely in this way. And, in the case of collective agents, let us agree that (b) they are *collectively* responsible for the choices they make when they make them freely. But, it will almost certainly be added, this is not enough to make any collective agents *morally* responsible for the free choices they make. At most, it will be said, it only makes them *socially* responsible for them, that is, answerable to the relevant community for them. The moral responsibility, it will be said, must be borne by the people who ultimately decide collectively what to do, and give the orders to do it.

There are two importantly different judgements that one may make concerning the freely made decisions. First, one may ask whether X is morally responsible for having decided to do Y. This is the question of whether X made the decision freely, and so must bear moral responsibility for it. Secondly, one may ask whether X's decision to do Y was a morally responsible one. And this is a question about the rightness of X's decision. Pettit's account of moral responsibility enables us to answer the first of these two questions. But it does not help us to answer the second. We shall return to consider this question in Chapter 7.

Social responsibility

Personal and collective responsibility are species of social responsibility. For, any answer to the question of whether X is personally or collectively responsible for doing Y is necessarily an answer to the question of whether X is socially responsible for doing Y. It is true that X is personally responsible for doing Y is often taken to imply that X is morally responsible for doing Y. But to whom, one may ask, is X morally responsible for doing anything? The old answer that we are morally responsible to God for what we do is clearly unsatisfactory, if one accepts a realist metaphysical theory. If the supposed custodian of the moral order is society, or its appointed system of justice, then there would appear to be no distinction to be drawn between moral and social responsibility. But surely we do wish to draw such a distinction. For, if we do not, or cannot do this, then we can have no basis for moral criticism of the social order. Therefore, the only plausible custodian of moral responsibility must be the individual or collective agent making the decision. But this too looks like a recipe for disaster. For it allows individual and collective agents to be judges in their own cause, and therefore to do what they sincerely believe to be morally right, independently of what anyone else might think. Consequently, however appalling their behaviour may be thought to be by others, it would appear to give them a licence to do it. A system that gives everyone the high moral ground effectively gives it to none.

There is, as far as I can see, only one way of avoiding this social disaster, and that is to deny morality its present high ground. Traditionally, our moral judgements have always been considered to be the dominant ones; so that if there is a conflict between what we think we are morally obliged to do, and what we are socially required to do, then the moral course of action should always triumph. The suggestion that this is not so is, of course, a radical one. Nevertheless, it turns out to be highly defensible. For if we think of morals as social ideals, we can easily account for the social value of moral criticism, without laying ourselves open to the charge of promoting moral anarchy. In these days of almost unlimited corporate power, and of militant religious fundamentalism, moral anarchy is almost the last thing we want. A well-ordered world needs to be able to suppress such forces without being accused of riding roughshod over people's moral sensitivities.

7

REALISM IN ETHICS

If the metaphysics of scientific realism is accepted as a first philosophy, then an acceptable moral theory must be one that is compatible with it. It cannot be a theory that depends on any kind of mental determinism that is incompatible with physical determinism. Nor can it be one that is not compatible with evolutionary theory. Human beings must be physically plausible systems. Nevertheless, it is a fact that I can decide what I want to do, and act on my decision. So, my coming to that decision must be achieved by a physical process, presumably meta-causal process, that establishes in me the disposition to act on some appropriate cue in the way that I have decided. Moreover, my acting on this decision must be an action that is triggered by the occurrence of this cue. It cannot be just a matter of chance that I happen to act in this way, given the occurrence of the cue. For then it would not be an act for which I was personally responsible. Similar conditions apply to acts of collective responsibility. For a group to decide collectively to act in some way, and act on that decision, it must first decide, by some appropriate deliberative procedure, what to do, on what occasion to do it, and then put in place a mechanism for triggering that decision. If these conditions are all satisfied, and the trigger occurs, then the group may be said to be collectively responsible to the action they have taken.

In what follows I shall assume that personal decision-making is like collective decision-making, except that it all takes place in one brain. Ideas may be floated, considered more or less imaginatively, argued for or against, and a decision made. Sometimes there is a predisposition to decide in one way rather than another, and a decision can be made very quickly, with little or no consideration. In any case, what is established or reinforced is a disposition to act on some appropriate cue. Among the considerations that may go into the making of a decision, there are some that would be considered to be moral, and others that would normally be regarded as self-interested, practical, legal or vengeful, as the case may be. Our interest here must be in the so-called "moral" considerations. What are they? What is their nature?

The main problem is that whatever they are, moral obligations are supposed to be capable of outweighing all other considerations, including those of self-interest, interests of friends and family, social obligations, legal obligations or even all of these combined. So, whatever they are, they must be very important. This is the traditional problem of dominance. What is it about moral obligations that makes them so imperative that they should dominate over all others? This problem has been one of the core problems of moral philosophy since the Enlightenment. In the religious ages that preceded the Enlightenment, there was a ready answer to this question. Our moral obligations are our obligations to God, and therefore must take precedence over all others. But with the decline of Christianity as the main influence in Western philosophy, this answer has largely ceased to be available; and for those to whom it remains available, it has ceased to be convincing, even to them. Very few Western philosophers nowadays would endorse the argument, and of those who would, most would concede that it is inconclusive.

Whatever position one takes on the dominance problem, there is no denying that moral theorists have made powerful critiques of many of our laws and social customs, for example in areas such as human rights, social and medical services, women's liberation, racial discrimination, animal welfare, gay and lesbian rights, and so on. So, presumably, we should aim to preserve this capacity in any new theory. For example, if the identification of morality with rationality were not too implausible, then, given the persuasive power of rational considerations, this would undoubtedly be a good argument for such a moral theory. But, despite some notable attempts to construct such a rationalist theory of morality, no such identification has much plausibility.

Christine Korsgaard (1996) and Michael Smith (1994) have, nevertheless, both argued for a purely rational foundations of morality.[1] If their arguments were sound, they would presumably establish that any rational person would have to endorse a humanist principle of intrinsic human value. Korsgaard does so explicitly, and Smith is surely committed to doing so. But then, I am deeply puzzled about what the status of this principle would have to be for this to be true. If being intrinsically valuable were of the essence of humanity, then the principle that human beings are intrinsically valuable would be metaphysically necessary. But is this so? Korsgaard argues that human beings are (a) essentially rational agents, (b) bound to value being human beings, and hence the property or set of properties in virtue of which they are human, and therefore (c) bound to value anyone, or anything else, that has this property.

But, *prima facie*, this is implausible. First, human beings are not members of a natural kind in the strict sense of "natural kind" used in essentialist theory. Human beings are members of what I call a "cluster kind". Cluster kinds are like natural kinds, but have looser criteria for kind membership. Human beings are distinguished as a species from other current species by the broad structure of their genomes. But, as we go back in history, the structure of the human genome is thought to become less and less distinct from that of our closest non-human relatives. Secondly, it is not an essential property of being human that one should value being human, and certainly not an essential property of being human that one should value the structure of the human genome. If human beings could be rid of their hatred for other human beings by a little bit of genetic modification, then I would be all in favour of it. But, perhaps the contention is not that the humanist principle is metaphysically necessary, but rather that it is analytic. In that case, however, this principle is just the claim that nothing would be *called* "human", if it were not intrinsically valuable. Maybe this is true. But if it were, anti-humanists would just have

---

1. I am grateful to Norva Lo for her insightful discussions of these neo-Kantian positions.

to stop calling people "human" if they did not consider them to be intrinsically valuable. Unfortunately, there is much gruesome precedence for doing just this.

The time has come, I think, to begin to explore the possibility of constructing a non-dominance theory of morality, that is, a theory in which moral considerations are just some among others of those involved in rational decision-making. For no one, in over two hundred years since Kant wrote the *Grundlegung*, has succeeded in developing a metaphysically satisfactory dominance theory of morality, for example of the kind sought by Korsgaard and Smith. Yet the task is not hopeless. For there is at least one kind of consideration that is potentially powerful socially, but which is not dominant in the required way, namely, our response to the question: What would you ideally like to see happen in such cases? The theory to which I refer is that of morality as social ideal. I call it the "social ideal theory of morality". However, to articulate this theory, it is necessary to make a small diversion into social contract theory. For the idealization required is of the relevant section of the social contract concerning the kinds of actions that we are considering.

De facto social contracts

There are many different views about the position and role of social contracts in moral and political theory. According to one tradition, that of Hobbes and Locke, the social contract of a society should be thought of as its founding document: an agreement forged in the state of nature to establish a system of government that defines the rights and responsibilities of its members, of its sovereign body and of its principal institutions. But, according to another tradition, that of Rousseau and Marx, the aim of all progressive politics should be to replace a society's institutions and effective system of rights and obligations with better ones. This is the tradition to which this chapter belongs. If morality is a system of social ideals, the moral quest must be to promote these ideals, with a view to incorporating them as far as possible into the *de facto* social contracts of societies around the world.

The *de facto* social contract of a society is the historically generated settlement concerning the nature and structure of that society that defines the kinds of organizations it contains, and the kinds of positions or roles that people may have within it, or within any of its organizations. The *de facto* social contract of a society also describes the proper distribution of rights, responsibilities and obligations of organizations, and of individuals *vis-à-vis* their social positions or roles in society, or within any of its organizations. The *de facto* social contract of a society is thus a true, comprehensive, sociologically discoverable account of its structure and mode of operation. As such, it should state which classes of individuals, or which kinds of organizations, are held to be responsible for doing what in society. It should say what the members think they have a right to expect of its governments, business corporations, trade unions, universities, hospitals and so on. It should explain how professionals and tradespeople (i.e. doctors, nurses, plumbers, public servants, etc.) should behave in their respective roles. And it should state what the responsibilities are of its various classes of individual members (i.e. citizens, children, asylum seekers, pensioners, prisoners, warders, etc.), and what they must do to carry out their responsibilities.

From the point of view of an outside observer of the society, the text (if it were ever to be written down) of the *de facto* social contract would be purely descriptive. For it would just describe the society's structure and the normal roles of the various kinds of agents within this structure. However, from the point of view of an agent who is a member of the society, the statement would be normative. For every social agent in a society must know what they will normally be held responsible for doing, to whom they will be held responsible, and what they will be expected to do in the exercise of their responsibilities. Therefore, in the absence of special or exonerating circumstances, the agent must know what he, she or it should do as a responsible social agent in that society.

According to Hume, one can never derive an "ought" from an "is". So, no description of how society *is* organized can possibly tell us how it *ought* to be. This is true. Nevertheless, a full description of how rights and responsibilities are distributed in a society does tell us what the *prima facie social* rights and obligations of its various kinds of agents are *vis-à-vis* each other. Therefore, if you know what kind of social agent you are, and you know what social rights and responsibilities you have in virtue of being an agent of this kind in the society in which you live, then you must know what you ought, socially, to do. And, you will have these social obligations however you might think society ought ideally to be organized. You have them just in virtue of the fact that you have the social profile you have, and that your society has settled on this particular social agreement concerning people of your social profile.

But clearly, your social obligations do not determine your moral obligations. For, according to the social ideal theory that is to be developed here, what you take your moral obligations to be would have to depend on what principles of social behaviour you thought would be mandatory for people of your profile in an ideal society. Where the two were the same, there would be no moral dilemma. But where they differed, there would be. For, in every such case, the moral principles that you have accepted would conflict with your known social obligations. So, for you, the question would arise: should I act on principles that I believe to be morally sound, or should I act on principles that I know to be socially required? There is no easy answer. For what it would be reasonable for you to do would depend on how strongly you believed in the soundness of your moral judgement, how important you considered the moral issue to be, what penalties you would face for neglecting your social obligations and what the consequences for others would be of your defaulting. In practice, many of us would compromise. We might, for example, do as little as we can of what we are socially obliged to do, all the while protesting that it is unjust. Or, if we felt strong enough to resist the social pressures, we might do what we think we ought morally to do, and be prepared to take the consequences of breaching the social code. But it should not be assumed that our perceived moral obligations should always override our known social obligations, or vice versa. The "right-to-lifer" who blows up an abortion clinic to save the lives of unborn children does what she perceives to be her moral duty. But there is nothing noble about what she does. It is a violent and perhaps murderous act.

Hume is also famous for his claim that "Custom ... is the great guide to human life. It is that principle alone", he said, "which renders our experience useful to us, and makes us expect, for the future, a similar train of events with those which have appeared in the past" (Hume [1777] 1975: 44). I doubt this. But I do not deny that custom does generate rational expectations. Moreover, I think it has an important role in generating our *prima facie* social obligations, that is, the sorts of obligations that are built into our *de facto* social contract. For wherever it is (a) a normal and socially approved expectation that we should behave in the manner X in circumstances of the kind Y, and (b) that other people need to know for practical reasons what we will do if we should find ourselves in circumstances of the kind Y, we naturally have a *prima facie* obligation to act in the manner X. The well-being of others, perhaps a great many others, may depend on it. The obligation arises because we are, in fact, all necessarily dependent on the actions and testimonies of others, and the sole basis on which we have to judge who is reliable, or what we can expect to be done in given circumstances, is how individuals, or people in various social roles, have behaved in the past.

If A lies to us in circumstances in which we can normally expect A to be telling the truth, and, as a result, we act in a way that is harmful to others, then A must bear a large share of the responsibility for their suffering. It does not matter that there was never any verbal or written agreement that A would tell the truth. For the fact is that we were relying on A to give us true information, and had good reason to expect A to do so. When the president of the United States, and the prime ministers of Great Britain and Australia took their countries to war in Iraq on the basis of intelligence that they had good reason to believe was faulty, but pretended that it was beyond reasonable doubt that Iraq was rapidly developing a nuclear weapons capability, they effectively lied to their people, and took them to war on false pretences. In doing so, all three behaved in ways directly contrary to the *de facto* social contracts of their societies. For we all had a social contractual right to expect our political leaders to speak frankly and honestly about the reasons for such a grave decision. It is part of what is known as the "Westminster system of ministerial responsibility", which, until then, was widely respected almost everywhere in the English-speaking world. But the actions of these three leaders undermined this understanding, and so weakened the social fabrics of their respective societies.

But the obligations arising through custom all seem to be just *prima facie* social obligations, not moral duties. The question, then, is how social obligations can become converted into moral obligations.

The thesis to be defended here is that our moral obligations are just the (actual or possible) social ones that we suppose would have to be made binding on all agents within the relevant classes in any ideal society. The social obligations we actually have are those that arose out of the historical processes that generated the *de facto* social contract of our own society. The moral obligations that we now have are those social obligations that we do or might have that would be binding on all agents within the relevant classes in any ideal society in which the same kinds of actions could be performed in the same kinds of circumstances. The obligation to do what we think we are morally obliged to do is therefore not just contingent on the social contract of the society in which we happen to live; it is a social obligation that we think would be binding on us in any ideal society. But, since our own society falls short of being an ideal one, it is not binding in our own society. Nor is there any guarantee that what we think ought to be binding in any ideal society will be strongly endorsed by most others. Our first duty as a moral reformer is to take whatever steps we think are both necessary and desirable to move the actual society in the direction of becoming what we conceive to be the ideal one in the hope that the ideal will take root in people's consciences, and lead to a movement in the direction in which we believe society ought to be moved.

A social moral theory for a given society may thus be one that is based on an idealization of the society's *de facto* social contract. If so, then the question that moral philosophers must ask is: what kind of idealization is required to maximally enhance the quality of life (if this is your primary value) of those living in your society? And, your answer to this question will define what I call "your social moral stance". It will, by implication, define your position on some of the moral issues that are to be faced in your society. But your position on many other issues is likely to remain undefined. For, it is unlikely that you, or anyone else, could complete the task of developing an ideal social contract for the whole of society.

A social moral theory, as I conceive it, is a form of utilitarianism. But it is new to the literature, as far as I know. It is, as we shall see, manifestly different from both act and rule utilitarianism. For what has to be evaluated for utility is not any particular action or rule, but a comprehensive set of norms defining the rights, obligations and

responsibilities of each of the different kinds of social agents existing in the ideal society. Let us call this kind of moral theory "social
contractual utilitarianism", in order to distinguish it from all of the
other varieties. It is a theory that fairly obviously makes quality of
life, rather than pleasure or happiness, the principal utilitarian value.
And the social rules that one would envisage as holding in one's ideal
society would have to apply to kinds of social agents, rather than just
to people generally. But, before developing the theory, we first need
to say something about the variety of kinds of social agents existing
in a modern society, and the inevitably complex structure of the *de
facto* social contract for any such society.

The variety of kinds of social agents

I use the term "social agent" to refer to anyone or any organization
that is capable of choosing freely how to act on matters of social concern, and of implementing their decisions. Thus, governments, police
forces, armies, corporations, schools, law courts, and fire brigades are
all social agents by this definition. The same is true of most individuals
in society. For they too are free to choose the courses of action they
wish to take, and of acting on their decisions. Accordingly, I lump
them all together in the general category of social agents.

Naturally, the *de facto* social contract of a society has very little
to say about the rights, obligations, responsibilities and powers of
social agents generally. For the different kinds of social agents have
very little in common, except the capacities to choose freely what to
do, and to act on their decisions. But there are some things that we
think no social agent in any society has a right to do, and these global constraints on what people, corporations and governments may
do are now being recognized, and built into the *de facto* social contracts of more and more societies. I refer specifically to the growing
body of international law concerning human rights, the dispropor-
tionate use of force, torture, genocide and so on. The enactment of
these laws, we might reasonably hope, is just the beginning of a process of incorporating what we take to be the core principles of the
moral law into the *de facto* social contracts of societies throughout
the world.

These global laws, fundamentally important as they are, do not feature strongly in the *de facto* social contracts of most societies. For the various kinds of social agents within any given society differ so widely in their powers, capacities, skills, spheres of influence and so on, that differences in their rights, obligations and responsibilities must be recognized. This is obvious, even at the individual level. The rights, obligations and responsibilities of adult citizens differ from those of children, non-citizens, asylum seekers, prison inmates and the insane. Those of surgeons, schoolteachers, geriatric nurses, plumbers, builders and bankers differ from each other, and from those who are none of these things. At the organizational level it is no less evident. The rights, obligations and responsibilities of national governments are different from those of regional or local governments, and those of all governments are different fundamentally from those of small businesses, large corporations, universities, hospitals, government departments, and non-governmental organizations, just as these are all different from each other. And these broad classifications may all be split in various ways to reveal a more fine-grained structure of rights, obligations and responsibilities. Inevitably, the *de facto* social contracts of most societies must be concerned with all of these details, and the social rights, obligations and responsibilities of individuals and organizations must be fine-tuned to these varying roles and profiles. The problem of developing a social contract for a whole society is inevitably made even more complex by the fact that classes of individuals and organizations are not natural kinds. Therefore, it is possible to envisage many different cross-categorizations of social agents, and consequently *de facto* social contracts operating in different societies that are fundamentally incommensurable with each other.

Rights, obligations, responsibilities and powers

To develop a system of morality, it is necessary to define the key concepts of moral discourse: rights, obligations, responsibilities and powers. The following definitions of these attributes are coherentist, not truth-conditional. They are coherentist in the sense that it would be irrational for any member of the relevant society who accepts the social ideals proposed to accept any definiendum and reject its definiens, or conversely. As such, they are definitions of the kind required for subjective probability theory, where truth does not come into it. But this need not concern us here. After all, the kind of meta-ethical theory that is being developed here is manifestly a subjectivist one. And, these are precisely the kinds of definitions required for such a theory.

Let us begin with the concept of an *ideal society*. A society is ideal for the purpose of judging what possible social obligations should be considered to be morally binding if and only if the utility of its *de facto* social contract is at least as great as that of any other possible society in which agents, actions and circumstances of the relevant kinds exist. (Note that this definition is intended to leave it an open question of what specific good is to be promoted. That is the subject for a moral theory, not just for a theory of moral rights, obligations, and so on, which is what we are concerned with here.)

Social rights and obligations

1. *A* prima facie *social obligation*: *x* has a *prima facie* social obligation to do Y in circumstances of the kind K, if *x* is a member of a class X of social agents all of whom would normally be required by the *de facto* social contract of the society to do Y in circumstances of the kind K.

2. *A* prima facie *social right*: *x* has a *prima facie* social right to Y in circumstances of the kind K if there is some social agent *z* who has a *prima facie* social obligation to realize Y in these circumstances.

3. *A social obligation*: *x* has a social obligation to do Y in circumstances of the kind K, if *x* has a *prima facie* social obligation to do Y in these circumstances, and there are no good and sufficient reasons why *x* should not be held to be socially accountable.

4. *A social right*: *x* has a social right to Y in circumstances of the kind K, if there is some agent *z* that has a social obligation to realize Y in these circumstances.

(Note that these definitions are cumulative: 4 depends on 3; and 2 and 3 depend on 1.)

Moral rights and obligations

5. *A prima facie moral obligation*: x has a *prima facie* moral obligation to do Y in circumstances of the kind K, if x is a member of a class X of social agents all of whom would have a *prima facie* social obligation to do Y in circumstances of the kind K in any ideal society.

6. *A prima facie moral right*: x has a *prima facie* moral right to Y in circumstances of the kind K, if there would be some social agent z, who would have a *prima facie* social obligation to realize Y in such circumstances in any ideal society.

7. *A moral obligation*: x has a moral obligation to do Y in circumstances of the kind K, if x is a social agent of the kind X, and, as such, x would have a social obligation to do Y in circumstances of this kind in any ideal society.

8. *A moral right*: x has a moral right to Y in circumstances of the kind K, if there would be some social agent z in an ideal society who would have a moral obligation to realize Y in such circumstances.

(Note that these definitions are also cumulative: 5 depends on 1; 6 depends on 5; 7 depends on 2; 8 depends on 7.)

Powers and responsibilities

The kinds of powers and responsibilities that are of interest to us here are those that can be given or taken away by a change in the *de facto* social contract. Let us call them social powers and responsibilities. Legal powers and responsibilities clearly fall into this category. A woman's power to conceive does not. But some of the social powers and responsibilities that exist in various societies are less formal than the legal ones, and less physical than the power to conceive. For there are powers and responsibilities that people have by default in the *de facto* social contracts of their societies. It may not be written into law that they have these powers and responsibilities. But they do, and they are expected to honour them. The responsibilities of parents for the care and protection of their children, for example, are presupposed in most societies. But, in cases where these responsibilities are deemed to have been neglected, the children may be taken away from their parents and put into foster care. So the responsibilities in these cases are default social responsibilities, and the powers of parents to exercise them, default social powers.

Social responsibilities are related to social obligations, but they are importantly different. Our social responsibilities are for making decisions in certain areas and acting on them. These areas are defined in the *de facto* social contract of our society, and our having these responsibilities necessarily involves our having social obligations to do what we believe to be for the best (i.e. for maximizing utility) in these areas. Here we define only the key concepts.

9. A prima facie *social responsibility*: x has a *prima facie* social responsibility for dealing with the issue Y, if and only if x has a *prima facie* social obligation to decide how best to deal with issue Y, and to act accordingly.

For example, parents can, in normal circumstances, decide how best to care for and protect their children under the age of maturity, and, as parents, they have a *prima facie* social obligation to implement their decisions on these matters. These are presumably the facts that we are expressing when we say that parents have *prima facie* social responsibilities to care and protect their children under mature age. However, the *de facto* social contract of our society does not rule the whole of our lives. It also provides for large areas in which we are free to choose for ourselves what to do. In these areas, we are still *prima facie* socially responsible for what we do. We are in fact *prima facie* socially responsible for everything that we choose to do in these areas. We should act for the best for all concerned. But in these areas, we are ourselves the ones who are mainly concerned.

Armed with the definition (9) of "*prima facie* social responsibility" it is a straightforward application of the theory of social contractual utilitarianism to derive the required definitions of "social responsibility", and of qualified (i.e. *prima facie*) and unqualified "moral responsibility". We can also proceed to define social and moral powers, although these terms are very rarely used. Here are the definitions of the key concepts.

10. *A social responsibility*: x has a social responsibility for dealing with issue Y, if and only if x has a social obligation to decide how best to deal with issue Y, and to act accordingly.

11. *A moral responsibility*: x has a moral responsibility for dealing with issue Y, if and only if x has a moral obligation to decide how best to deal with issue Y, and to act accordingly.

12. *A* prima facie *social power*: x has the *prima facie* social power to do Y if and only if, if x decides to do Y in the exercise of his/her/its responsibilities, then x has a *prima facie* social right to expect that this decision will be upheld by society and implemented.

Social contractual utilitarianism

The brand of social contractual utilitarianism that I favour for my own society is one that seeks to maximize human well-being, or *eudaimonia*, as the Greeks called it. In advocating this, I follow the lead of Amartya Sen and Martha Nussbaum. The theory advocates manipulating the system of rights, obligations, powers and responsibilities that are effective in our society with a view to maximizing human well-being. It might, for example, involve introducing a regime of regulation for corporate and other kinds of organizations with a view to making them more answerable to the general community for their actions. At present, these organizations mostly act within the law, but the law does very little to ensure that they act responsibly. Their freely chosen actions are, however, by no means socially irrelevant. On the contrary, the actions of large and powerful organizations in our community, such as banks, finance corporations, universities, hospitals, police forces and trade unions, to name just a few, probably do more to affect the lives and well-being of members of our society than all of the actions of individuals in pursuit of their own personal objectives combined. And some of them, as we have seen recently, are capable of doing immense harm on a global scale to people's well-being.

However, the form of social contractual utilitarianism that I should favour for my own society would not necessarily be appropriate for many other societies. It would not, for example, be appropriate for a society that is not governed by consent. For such a society has no *de facto* social contract to work with. The aim of promoting well-being must remain the same. But the strategy for achieving it must be varied. Accordingly, I take the view that to establish a moral order, we have first to establish a tolerable social order. For it is only when a society has reached this first stage of development that it can sensibly even begin the process of seeking to maximize human well-being by the fine-tuning processes of social regulation.

Social contractual utilitarianism is, of course, a bit like rule utilitarianism. For making changes to the regime of social rights, obligations, responsibilities and powers involves changing the rules, or changing the force with which they are upheld. But some changes to the rules may involve changes to the social structures within which they are formulated. A change in the rules to allow same sex marriages within the Catholic Church, for example, may involve many other changes to the *de facto* social contract that is effective in this society. And it is the impact on well-being that this set of changes would have that would have to be evaluated within the Church, before any decision is made.

Formally, social contractual utilitarianism is like Kantianism, since it involves thinking of moral principles as prospective laws for the society in which one lives. But the aim is not, as Kant's was, to construct the social contract for a society that is governed by *a priori* principles of rationality. It is, rather, to construct the social contract for an ideal society, that is, the one (if there is only one) that is empirically best suited to promoting human well-being as much as possible. It is also Kantian for the reason that it makes the proposed legislation primary, not any prior judgements that we may make about the rightness or wrongness of particular actions. It is just that the way of evaluating the rules is essentially different for a social contractual utilitarian. For a social contractual utilitarian, social rules must always be evaluated in a social context. Contextualization is necessary because the identity of any rule must always depend on that of the classificatory system that is used in the society, and the effects of implementing the rule must always be gauged by considering its effects, given the other rules that happen to be in place for agents and actions in this society.

Smart has argued that rule utilitarianism is irrational. He says that if a proposed rule requires one to act in a way that you know will have bad consequences overall, then it would be irrational for a utilitarian to act on this rule. But, for Smart, the primary objects of utilitarian evaluation are particular actions. For a rule utilitarian, they are kinds of actions. And, for a social contractual utilitarian, they are the principles of action for agents of various kinds within the existing social context. So, act utilitarians, rule utilitarians and social contractual utilitarians are all evaluating different things. The best act might not be in accord with the best rule, and the best rule might not be in accord with the best contractual arrangement. Smart and I are therefore a long way apart on this issue. Smart's position may reasonably be described as individualistic act utilitarianism. I believe this position to be an irrational one, as I shall now argue. If one's aim is to maximize utility, however utility might be defined, then the only rational strategy is to act on the best constructible social contract for maximizing utility.

Individualistic act utilitarianism

Given the definition (11) of "moral responsibility" above, Smart's position of individualistic act utilitarianism can easily be defined by deleting all reference to limiting or constraining circumstances from this definition, thus effectively insisting that all areas are ones in which we are all free to choose for ourselves what we ought to do that is for the best. That is, I assume that Smart's position may adequately be summed up: *Everyone has a moral responsibility to decide how best to deal with any issue (i.e. how to maximize utility for all concerned), and to act accordingly.*

Smart (1973: 12) argues that everyone has a moral obligation to act in such a way as to maximize probable benefit. For, he thinks, this is the best way to ensure that probable benefit will be maximized. I interpret Smart's term "the probable benefit of doing A" to mean what I mean by "the prospective utility of doing A", which is a function of the range of possible consequences of doing A, and their values. Suppose, for simplicity, that there are just two such mutually exclusive and jointly exhaustive consequences, C and −C, and let $V(C)$ and $V(-C)$ be their respective values. Then,

$$U(A) = V(C) \times P(C/A) + V(-C) \times P(-C/A)$$

That is, the utility of doing A is the sum of the values of the possible consequences of doing A, weighted according to the probabilities of their occurring, given that A is done. It is then readily demonstrable that if anyone were serious about trying to maximize utility in society as a whole, they would have to collaborate with like-minded people to distribute responsibilities for deciding what to do for the best, and be prepared to stick to this contractual arrangement. For the idea that prospective utility could be maximized otherwise is absurd. It is absurd because there are clear cases in which, according to this individualistic act utilitarian theory, X ought to do A, and Y ought to do B, even though, on the theory, and with the information available to all for them to do the necessary calculations, the prospective utility of the combination of actions, consisting of X doing A and Y doing B, is minimal. Hence, the theory would make it right for X and Y, as individuals, to do what, as a pair, they ought not, and know they ought not, to do. In these cases, the only way of dealing satisfactorily with the problem, from a utilitarian point of view, is for them to get together and decide what to do, and stick to this agreement. So, if your aim is to maximize utility, the prospective utilities of such contractual arrangements must be allowed to override the prospective utilities of individual choices. This is the only rational thing to do.

Consider two independently performable actions A and B of no intrinsic value, either of which could have the very good consequence C. Let the value of C, $V(C) = 100$, and the value of −C, $V(-C) = -100$. Suppose that A and B are both difficult things to do, and are therefore rarely done. Consistently with this assumption, let $P(A) = 0.11$, and $P(B) = 0.11$. However, A and B are actions that can interfere with each other and effectively prevent C from happening: $P(ABC) = 0$. But if A is done without B, or B is done without A, the results are quite likely to be good. Table 1, showing probability assignments and values, is one that is consistent with all of these assumptions.

Suppose now that X is in a position to do A, and that Y is in a position to do B. Then it follows from the table that if X and Y act rationally as individuals on the basis of the agreed values of C and −C, and the known probabilities of C and −C occurring (depending on what is done), then X will do A, and Y will do B (since $U(A) > U(-A)$, and $U(B) > U(-B)$).[2]

---

2. The case is different from the well-known Prisoners' Dilemma in several ways. First, the values in question are shared social values, not personal ones. That is, both A and B desire the outcome C, and abhor the outcome −C. Secondly,

But if X does A and Y does B, then we know, and X and Y must also know, that C will not occur. Moreover, they must know that this result is highly undesirable. What is required is that X and Y should do the opposite, that is, if X does A, then Y should not do B, or if X does not do A, then Y should do B. For these are the combinations of actions that are most likely to lead to the desired result C. However, the desired combination of actions can only be achieved either (a) by collaboration between X and Y, or (b) by one or other, but not both, of X and Y acting irrationally. The necessary conclusion is that if X and Y both wish to maximize utility, they must consult, decide together what to do and act accordingly.

There is no reason to think that the kind of situation represented in this proof is rare. On the contrary, it is rare that the probabilities of the consequences of our actions, and hence their prospective utilities, are independent of what other people do. Think of all of the ways that we can be acting at cross-purposes. And think how much more often we should find ourselves at cross-purposes with others if the only rule effectively guiding our behaviour were the general one: do whatever you think is for the best. Shouldn't we all try to help the most needy, for example, and consequently just get in each other's way? There is really only one way of dealing with this problem, which is to draw up a mini social contract to allocate responsibilities, and for all to be prepared to act according to this contract, unless there should be unforeseen circumstances that radically changes the situation. But to draw up such a social contract would really be to abandon individualistic act utilitarianism. For acceptance of it would create a range of *prima facie* social obligations, that is, obligations that we should socially bound to accept, unless there were overwhelming, and unforeseen, reasons for not doing so.

---

each person knows the probabilities of all of the relevant events; whereas, in the Prisoners' Dilemma, the probabilities are unknown, and irrelevant, since the argument is a dominance argument. Thirdly, if each person acts rationally on the basis of the calculated utilities, the result is the worst of all possible results. In the Prisoners' Dilemma, the rational decision to confess depends on adopting a strategy designed to avoid the worst possible result for the individual concerned. In this case, both are able to predict that the worst possible result (from both their points of view) will occur if they both act rationally on the basis of their shared beliefs and values.

Table 1. The incoherence of individualistic act utilitarianism.

Events	(a) Probabilities	(b) Values	(c) Derived probabilities of C	(d) Derived probabilities of −C	Utilities of outcomes $[U(x) = 100P(C/x) - 100P(-C/x)]$
ABC	0	100	$P(C/A) = 0.45$	$P(-C/A) = 0.55$	$U(A) = -10$
AB−C	.03	−100	$P(C/B) = 0.45$	$P(-C/B) = 0.55$	$U(B) = -10$
A−BC	.05	100	$P(C/AB) = 0$	$P(-C/AB) = 1$	$U(AB) = -100$
A−B−C	.03	−100	$P(C/-AB) = 0.62$	$P(-C/-AB) = 0.38$	$U(-AB) = 24$
−ABC	.05	100	$P(C/A-B) = 0.62$	$P(-C/A-B) = 0.38$	$U(A-B) = 24$
−AB−C	.03	−100	$P(C/-A-B) = 0.26$	$P(-C/-A-B) = 0.74$	$U(-A-B) = -48$
−A−BC	.21	100	$P(C/-A) = 0.29$	$P(-C/-A) = 0.71$	$U(-A) = -42$
−A−B−C	.60	−100	$P(C/-B) = 0.29$	$P(-C/-B) = 0.71$	$U(-B) = -42$

The limitations of social contractual theories of morality

Traditionally, moral theories have always been required to be quasi-universal in scope. In the English-speaking world, it has been widely held that moral principles must apply equally to all adult human beings, whatever their status, gender or education, provided only that they are capable of distinguishing between right and wrong. But a social contractual moral theorist cannot require so much. For moral knowledge is not *a priori*, and there is no reason to think that moral principles are so obvious or trivial that one would have to be too stupid, too young or legally insane to be ignorant of them. Social moral theorists must set their sights much lower than this. On the other hand, a good moral theory must deal adequately with the rights and responsibilities of collective and specialized agents. So, in this way, at least, it must be more ambitious than any traditional moral theory.

The crucial questions to ask are: what is the point of trying to develop a moral theory? What is it aiming to achieve? There have been many answers to these questions, and consequently many different ideas about what the motivation for morality must be. But, one who accepts scientific realism as a first philosophy cannot plausibly accept that it is (a) rational or long-term self-interest, (b) belief in a set of commands given to us by a god, or (c) the desire to live one's life by the natural light of reason. The only realistic candidate for the role of motivating principle would appear to be a social one, namely, the desire to create a better society, in which people can live better, happier, more fulfilling lives, where the natural and urban environments are well cared for, and where there are prevailing attitudes of fairness and generosity. We should be motivated to achieve such a goal, a social theorist may well argue, not only for our own (and other's) well-being, but also for that of our children and grandchildren. Ultimately we should aim to achieve such outcomes everywhere, so that everyone can benefit from our efforts.

However, the global ethical problem has special difficulties. For a great many societies are not governed by consent, and therefore do not have the sorts of *de facto* social contracts that consensual societies have. In many of these societies, the rules by which they operate have been imposed by the strong on the weak to serve their own interests. In others, they have been designed by clerics to pay homage to the gods they allegedly serve. Consequently, there may be no social ideals of the kind envisaged here that could plausibly be based on the traditions of such societies, and there may be much work to be done in many of them, before any sort of moral project could get under way. Nevertheless, it should be possible to work towards establishing consensual governments in such societies, and to assist them in their task of governing in the interests of their people. The governments required need not, and probably should not, all be Western-style adversarial democracies. Adversarial democracies are wasteful luxuries that the world can probably no longer afford. But they do need to be governments that operate with the consent of the governed.

The idea that moral principles are social ideals is not new. What is new is that the theory that has been developed is not based on the conception of an ideally rational society, but on that of a society that is ideally structured and regulated from the point of view of its members to maximize their well-being. In such a society, its competent members would all need to be well motivated to this end, and its forms of government, organizations, institutions, corporations and so on, adequately administered for this purpose. Presumably, there would also need to be a degree of regulation of the society's professionals, tradespeople, managers and people in various other social categories. In short, the ideal society would need to have a *de facto* social contract that defined the social roles, rights and obligations of its various classes of social agents. The thesis I wish to defend is that a theory of morality should ideally be about the ideal content of such a contract.

According to H. A. Prichard, a moral obligation (and therefore a moral right) has no nature that is capable of being expressed in terms of the nature of anything else: "it is *sui generis*", he said ([1937] 1949: 94). Prichard must have seemed at the time to have made a good case for this claim. For none of the analyses he considered does justice to the concept of moral obligation that we have inherited from our forebears. But his argument really only shows one of two things: either (a) that none of the many analyses that had been proposed over the years (i.e. pre-1937) was up to the job, or (b) that the concept of a moral obligation was itself in need of revision. I take the latter view. Our moral obligations have traditionally been understood as being ones that should override our social obligations. I am arguing here that in a consensual society, where there is conflict between the law and one's own moral judgement, obedience to the law should normally take precedence. A proposed moral law may challenge the law of the land in a consensual society, but it has no privileged status, and the right to act on it has to be fought for.

The merits of social contractual utilitarianism

To my knowledge, social contractual utilitarianism is the only moral theory that can cope adequately with the principal moral problems of advanced capitalist societies. For these problems centre on the powers and responsibilities of corporations, their management structures and the professionals associated with them. These are problems that are generally considered under the headings of "applied ethics" or "applied philosophy", names suggesting that they are not really issues of basic importance. But in the view that has been urged throughout this chapter, the opposite is the case. The most fundamental problem of moral theory is how to deal with the most powerful, and potentially some of the most constructive and destructive social agents in the modern world. Moreover, they are not the only such agents that have been ignored in mainstream ethics. Universities, armies, police forces, hospitals, and dozens of other collective agents have been systematically ignored in mainstream moral theory. To make matters worse, studies of technical and professional ethics have also been marginalized.

The reasons for this are easy to see. According to most present-day moral theorists, the only true bearers of moral rights, obligations and responsibilities are individuals. For, since the Enlightenment, nearly every moral philosopher has assumed that the source of all such moral properties or attributes must lie somehow in human nature. But, as they discovered to their distress, there is no easy way of founding a theory of morality on human nature. In the view that is being developed here, there is certainly a connection between the two. But it is very indirect. Ultimately, the kind of society that we find congenial, and supportive of what we take to be the most valuable things in life, depends on our common human nature. So human nature is not out of the picture. But it should no longer be so prominent in our thinking. So-called applied ethics must now take centre stage, and the focus must be on the powers, rights and responsibilities of the collective and specialized agents, which are the primary sources of good and evil in modern society.

The task of developing a moral theory adequate for all of the branches of ethics that have been neglected in the mainstream is a huge one; it is certainly beyond the capacity of any one moral philosopher to accomplish. But it is no longer so difficult to approach the problem. If social powers, rights and responsibilities belong directly to classes of social agents, as social contractual utilitarianism implies, then there is no need to explain how these powers, rights and responsibilities derive from those of individuals. There is nothing to explain. In fact, one can just start at the other end, and say what the powers, rights and responsibilities of collective and specialized agents are, or ought ideally to be, and then figure out ways of making the specialists, or individuals who are engaged in the collectives, responsible for achieving the required outcomes. Plausibly, the first step should be to categorize the various collective and specialized agents, draw up charters for each of the categories, and go through a ratification and approval process for the charters. The second step should then be to make the specialists and the company directors, or other individuals in charge of collective agencies (vice chancellors, archbishops and so on), sign off on the approved charters, and hold them personally and legally responsible for adhering to them.

Objections

One objection to the social contractual utilitarianism is likely to be that it leads to a pernicious form of ethical relativism. For people with different religious, cultural or social backgrounds are likely to have very different conceptions of the ideal society, and very different ideas about the good that the ideal social contract should aim to promote. For some, the primary good might be some kind of piety. This might, for example, be the case for a devoutly Muslim country. Moreover, the societies of these countries could conceivably be consensual; that is, the people who live in them might, by and large, be accepting of the styles of government and the laws and social mores that exist there.

Should we, then, just turn a blind eye to the social injustices that, from our perspective, exist in these countries? Should we, for example, ignore behaviour that we see as involving gross abuse of women? Or should we, rather, try to persuade them that their values are all wrong? I think we should. We should try to persuade them as hard as we can that their attitudes are both cruel and unjust. And, if they in return should try to persuade us that our values are bad, then let them. We should welcome the debate, and hope to learn from it. We must engage in dialogue with those with whom we disagree morally, I would say, because our ultimate aim has to be to establish a global consensus on rights, obligations, powers and responsibilities, that is, a global morality. No such consensus now exists. But it is probably a necessary condition for the global harmony and cooperation that nearly everyone seeks.

Another objection to the social contractual theory of morality is one that is more likely to be felt than openly stated. It is that the social idealism on which it depends has a very bad name. It is a term that immediately conjures up images of communism, fascism and Wahhabism, and suggests that any theory that depends on it must inevitably lead to violence of the kinds associated with such positions. But there is nothing intrinsically revolutionary or reactionary about the theory of moral obligation that has been developed in this chapter. What would be revolutionary would be an attempt by a dictator, or by a government that is entrenched in power, to impose his or her, or its, vision of an ideal society directly and uncompromisingly on an existing social democracy, thus riding roughshod over the historical processes of adjustment and accommodation that would normally occur. For any social ideal that really met human needs would have to be one that was fine-tuned to the complexities of human social arrangements, and to the diversity of human beliefs and values. The *de facto* social contracts of the best societies in the world are not ones that have been imposed on reluctant citizens by revolutionary force, but ones that have been arrived at by the slow historical processes of social adaptation. And there is good reason to think that this will always be the case. The best societies are not created by zealots; their social contracts have all evolved to take full account of people's diverse attitudes and changing concerns. Moral crusades, on the other hand, intended to create whole new social structures, are nearly always bad news. This point was made long ago by Edmund Burke ([1910] 1953) when he was commenting on the French Revolution. No one, he argued, can construct an ideal social contract from scratch. For no one has, or could have, the necessary wisdom or experience to do so. The best that we as individuals can do is just to propose some moral guidelines, and do what we can to persuade others to accept them as social principles.

BIBLIOGRAPHY

Armstrong, D. M. 1983. *What is a Law of Nature?* Cambridge: Cambridge University Press.

Armstrong, D. M. 1997. *A World of States of Affairs*. Cambridge: Cambridge University Press.

Armstrong, D. M. 1999a. "Comment on Ellis". In *Causation and Laws of Nature*, H. Sankey (ed.), 43–8. Dordrecht: Kluwer.

Armstrong, D. M. 1999b. "The Causal Theory of Properties: Properties According to Shoemaker, Ellis and Others". *Philosophical Topics* **26**: 25–37.

Armstrong, D. M. 2002. "Two Problems for Essentialism". In *The Philosophy of Nature: A Guide to the New Essentialism*, B. D. Ellis, 167–71. Chesham: Acumen.

Bigelow, J. C. 1988. *The Reality of Numbers: A Physicalist's Philosophy of Mathematics*. Oxford: Clarendon Press.

Bigelow, J. C. 1999. "Scientific Ellisianism". In *Causation and Laws of Nature*, H. Sankey (ed.), 45–59. Dordrecht: Kluwer.

Bigelow, J. C., B. D. Ellis & C. E. Lierse 1992. "The World as One of a Kind; Natural Necessity and Laws of Nature". *British Journal for the Philosophy of Science* **43**: 371–88.

Bird, A. 2005. "Laws and Essences". *Ratio: Special Issue on Metaphysics in Science* **18**: 437–61.

Bitbol, M. 2007. "Schrödinger Against Particles and Quantum Jumps". In *Quantum Mechanics at the Crossroads*, J. Evans & A. Thorndike (eds), 81–106. Berlin: Springer.

Bohm, D. 1952. "A Suggested Interpretation of Quantum Theory in Terms of Hidden Variables". *Physical Review* **85**: 166–93.

Born, M. 1949. *Natural Philosophy of Cause and Chance*. Oxford: Oxford University Press.

Bradley, F. H. [1876] 1959. "My Station and Its Duties". In *Ethical Studies*, 2nd edn, 160–213. Oxford: Clarendon Press.

Bridgman, P. W. [1927] 1954. *The Logic of Modern Physics*. New York: Macmillan

Bridgman, P. W. 1963. *A Sophisticate's Primer of Relativity*. London: Routledge & Kegan Paul.

Burke, E. [1910] 1953. *Reflections on the French Revolution*, A. J. Grieve (intro.). London: Dent.

Campbell, N. R. 1957. *Foundations of Science: The Philosophy of Theory and Experiment*. New York: Dover. Originally published as *Physics: The Elements* (Cambridge: Cambridge University Press, 1921).

Carnap, R. 1963. "Adolf Grünbaum on the Philosophy of Space and Time". In *The Philosophy of Rudolf Carnap*, by P. A. Schilpp (ed.). LaSalle, IL: Open Court.

Carroll, J. W. 1994. *Laws of Nature*. Cambridge: Cambridge University Press.

Cartwright, N. 1979. "Causal Laws and Effective Strategies". *Noûs* **13**: 419–37. Reprinted in her *How the Laws of Physics Lie*, ch. 1 (Oxford: Oxford University Press, 1983).

Cartwright, N. 1983. *How the Laws of Physics Lie*. Oxford: Oxford University Press.

Cartwright, N. 1989. *Nature's Capacities and their Measurement*. Oxford: Oxford University Press.

Churchland, P. M. 1979. *Scientific Realism and the Plasticity of Mind*. Cambridge: Cambridge University Press.

Churchland, P. M. & C. Hooker (eds) 1985. *Images of Science: Essays on Realism and Empiricism, With a Reply from Bas C. Van Fraassen*. Chicago, IL: University of Chicago Press.

Clarke, R. 2005. "On an Argument for the Impossibility of Moral Responsibility". In *Midwest Studies in Philosophy, vol. 29: Free Will and Moral Responsibility*, P. A. French, H. K. Wettstein & J. M. Fischer (eds), 13–24. Oxford: Blackwell.

Colodny, R. G. (ed.) 1965. *Beyond the Edge of Certainty: Essays in Contemporary Science and Philosophy*. Englewood Cliffs, NJ: Prentice-Hall.

Descartes, R. [1637] 1954. *Discourse on the Method of Rightly Conducting One's Reason and of Seeking Truth in the Sciences*, E. Anscombe & P. Geach (eds & trans.). In *Descartes: Philosophical Writings*, 5–58. Edinburgh: Thomas Nelson.

Devitt, M. 1984. *Realism and Truth*, 2nd. rev. edn. Oxford: Blackwell.

Dowe, P. 2000. *Physical Causation*. Cambridge: Cambridge University Press.

Dowe, P. & P. Noordhof (eds) 2004. *Cause and Chance: Causation in an Indeterministic World*. London: Routledge.

Duhem, P. 1954. *The Aim and Structure of Physical Theory*, P. P. Wiener (trans.). Princeton, NJ: Princeton University Press.

Einstein, A. 1909. "Über die Entwicklung unserer Anschauung über das Wesen und die Konstitution der Strahlung". *Physickalische Zeitschrift* **10**: 817–25.

Ellis, B. D. 1957. "A Comparison of Process and Non-process Theories in the Physical Sciences". *British Journal for the Philosophy of Science* **29**: 45–56.

Ellis, B. D. 1965. "The Origin and Nature of Newton's Laws of Motion". In *Beyond the Edge of Certainty*, R. G. Colodny (ed.), 29–68. Englewood Cliffs, NJ: Prentice Hall.

Ellis, B. D. 1966. *Basic Concepts of Measurement*. Cambridge: Cambridge University Press.

Ellis, B. D. 1971. "On Conventionality and Simultaneity: A Reply". *Australasian Journal of Philosophy* **49**: 177–203.

Ellis, B. D. 1976. "The Existence of Forces". *Studies in the History and Philosophy of Science* **7**: 171–85.

Ellis, B. D. 1979. *Rational Belief Systems*. Oxford: Blackwell.

Ellis, B. D. 1980. "Truth as a Mode of Evaluation". *Pacific Philosophical Quarterly* **1**: 85–99.

Ellis, B. D. 1985. "What Science Aims to Do". In *Images of Science: Essays on Realism and Empiricism, With a Reply by Bas C. Van Fraassen*, P. Churchland & C. Hooker (eds), 166–93. Chicago, IL: University of Chicago Press.

Ellis, B. D. 1987. "The Ontology of Scientific Realism". In *Metaphysics and Morality: Essays in Honour of J. J. C. Smart*, P. Pettit, R. Sylvan & J. Norman (eds), 50–70. Oxford: Blackwell.

Ellis, B. D. 1988a. "Solving the Problem of Induction using a Values-based Epistemology". *British Journal for the Philosophy of Science* **39**: 141–60.

Ellis, B. D. 1988b. "Internal Realism". *Synthese* **76**: 409–34.

Ellis, B. D. 1990. *Truth and Objectivity*. Oxford: Blackwell.

Ellis, B. D. 2001. *Scientific Essentialism*. Cambridge: Cambridge University Press.

Ellis, B. D. 2002. *The Philosophy of Nature: A Guide to the New Essentialism*. Chesham: Acumen.

Ellis, B. D. 2005a. "Physical Realism". *Ratio* **18**: 371–84.

Ellis, B. D. 2005b. "Marc Lange on Essentialism". *Australasian Journal of Philosophy* **83**: 75–9.

Ellis, B. D. 2005c. "Katzav on the Limitations of Dispositionalism". *Analysis* **65**: 90–92.

Ellis, B. D. 2005d. "Universals, the Essential Problem, and Categorical Properties". *Ratio: Special Issue on Metaphysics in Science* **18**: 462–72.

Ellis, B. D. & P. Bowman 1967. "Conventionality in Distant Simultaneity". *Philosophy of Science* **34**: 116–36.

Ellis, B. D. & C. E. Lierse 1994. "Dispositional Essentialism". *Australasian Journal of Philosophy* **72**: 27–45.

Evans, J. & A. S. Thorndike (eds) 2007. *Quantum Mechanics at the Crossroads*. Berlin: Springer.

Everett, H. 1957. "'Relative State' Formulation of Quantum Mechanics". *Reviews of Modern Physics* **29**: 452–64.

Fales, E. 1990. *Causation and Universals*. London: Routledge & Kegan Paul.

Feyerabend, P. 1965. "Problems of Empiricism". In *Beyond the Edge of Certainty: Essays in Contemporary Science and Philosophy*, R. G. Colodny (ed.), 145–260. Englewood Cliffs, NJ: Prentice-Hall.

Fine, A. 1984. "The Natural Ontological Attitude". In *Scientific Realism*, J. Leplin (ed.), 83–107. Berkeley, CA: University of California Press.

Forrest, P. 1986. *The Dynamics of Belief*. Oxford: Blackwell.

Forrest, P. 1994. "Why Most of Us Should be Scientific Realists: A Reply to van Fraassen". *Monist* 77: 47–70.

Fox, J. F. 1987. "Truthmaker". *Australasian Journal of Philosophy* 65: 188–207.

Freedman, D. Z. & P. van Nieuwenhuizen 1978. "Supergravity and the Unification of the Laws of Physics". *Scientific American* 239 (February): 126–43.

French, P. A., H. K. Wettstein & J. M. Fischer (eds) 2005. *Midwest Studies in Philosophy, vol. 29: Free Will and Moral Responsibility*. Oxford: Blackwell.

Frisch, M. 2000. "(Dis-)Solving the Puzzle of the Arrow of Radiation". *British Journal of the Philosophy of Science* 51: 381–410.

Frisch, M. 2005. *Inconsistency, Asymmetry and Non-locality: Philosophical Issues in Classical Electrodynamics*. New York: Oxford University Press.

Gauthier, D. 1986. *Morals by Agreement*. Oxford: Oxford University Press.

Gauthier, D. 1991. "Why Contractarianism?". In *Contractarianism and Rational Choice*, P. Vallentyne (ed.), 15–30. Cambridge: Cambridge University Press.

Grünbaum, A. 1973. *Philosophical Problems of Space and Time*, 2nd enlarged edn, Boston Studies in the Philosophy of Science, 12. Dordrecht: Reidel.

Grünbaum, A., W. Salmon, B. C. Van Fraassen & A. Janis 1969. "Panel Discussion of Simultaneity by Slow Clock Transport in the Special and General Theories of Relativity". *Philosophy of Science* 36: 1–81.

Handfield, T. 2001. "Dispositional Essentialism and the Possibility of a Law-abiding Miracle". *Philosophical Quarterly* 51: 484–94.

Handfield, T. 2008. "Humean Dispositionalism". *Australasian Journal of Philosophy* 86: 113–26.

Handfield, T. 2009. "The Metaphysics of Dispositions and Causes". In *Dispositions and Causes*, T. Handfield (ed.), 1–30. Oxford: Oxford University Press.

Harré, R. & E. H. Madden 1975. *Causal Powers: A Theory of Natural Necessity*. Oxford: Blackwell.

Heathcote, A. 1984. "Causal Theories of Space and Time". Unpublished PhD thesis, La Trobe University, Melbourne.

Heil, J. 2003. *From an Ontological Point of View*. Oxford: Clarendon Press.

Heil, J. 2005. "Kinds and Essences". *Ratio: Special Issue on Metaphysics in Science* 18: 405–19.

Helmholtz, H. von [1847] 1935. "On the Conservation of Force", J. Tyndall (trans.). In *A Source Book of Physics*, W. F. Magie (ed.), 212–20. New York: McGraw-Hill.

Hume, D. [1777] 1975. *Enquiry Concerning Human Understanding*, P. H. Nidditch (ed.). Oxford: Clarendon Press.

Jackson, F. C. 1998. *From Metaphysics to Ethics: A Defence of Conceptual Analysis*. Oxford: Oxford University Press.

Katzav, J. 2004. "Dispositions and the Principle of Least Action". *Analysis* 64: 206–14.

Korsgaard, C. 1996. *The Sources of Normativity*. Cambridge: Cambridge University Press.

Kukla, A. 1994. "Scientific Realism, Scientific Practice, and the Natural Ontological Attitude". *British Journal for the Philosophy of Science* **45**: 955–75.

Ladyman, J. 1998. "What is Structural Realism?". *Studies in the History and Philosophy of Science* **29**: 409–24.

Ladyman, J. & D. Ross 2007. *Every Thing Must Go: Metaphysics Naturalized*. Oxford: Oxford University Press.

Lange, M. 2004. "A Note on Scientific Essentialism, Laws of Nature and Counterfactual Conditionals". *Australasian Journal of Philosophy* **82**: 227–41.

Laudan, L. 1981. "A Confutation of Convergent Realism". *Philosophy of Science* **48**: 19–49.

Leplin, J. (ed.) 1984. *Scientific Realism*. Berkeley, CA: University of California Press.

Lewis, D. K. 1973. *Counterfactuals*. Cambridge, MA: Harvard University Press.

Lewis, D. K. 1986. "Against Structural Universals". *Australasian Journal of Philosophy* **64**: 25–46.

Lowe, E. J. 1998. *The Possibility of Metaphysics: Substance, Identity and Time*. Oxford: Clarendon Press.

Lowe, E. J. 2002. *A Survey of Metaphysics*. Oxford: Oxford University Press.

Martin, C. B. 1993a. "The Need for Ontology: Some Choices". *Philosophy* **68**: 505–22.

Martin, C. B. 1993b. "Powers for Realists". In *Ontology, Causality and Mind: Essays in Honour of D. M. Armstrong*, J. Bacon, K. K. Campbell & L. Reinhardt (eds), 175–94. Cambridge: Cambridge University Press.

Martin, C. B. 1994. "Dispositions and Conditionals". *Philosophical Quarterly* **44**: 1–8.

Martin, C. B. 1997. "On the Need for Properties: The Road to Pythagoreanism and Back". *Synthese* **112**: 193–221.

Maxwell, J. C. 1881. *Elementary Treatise on Electricity*, William Garnett (ed.). Oxford: Clarendon Press.

McCall, S. 1994. *A Model of the Universe: Space–Time, Probability, and Decision*. Oxford: Clarendon Press.

Mehlberg, H. 1961. "Physical Laws and Time's Arrow". In *Current Issues in the Philosophy of Science*, H. Feigl & G. Maxwell (eds), 105–38. New York: Holt, Reinhardt & Winston.

Mele, A. R. 1995. *Autonomous Agents: From Self-control to Autonomy*. New York: Oxford University Press.

Molnar, G. 1999. "Are Dispositions Reducible?". *Philosophical Quarterly* **49**: 1–17.

Molnar, G. 2003. *Powers: A Study in Metaphysics*, S. Mumford (ed.). Oxford: Oxford University Press.

Mumford, S. D. 2004. *Laws in Nature*. London: Routledge.

Mumford, S. D. 2005. "Kinds, Essences, Powers". *Ratio: Special Issue on Metaphysics in Science* **18**: 420–36.

Musgrave, A. 1999. *Essays on Realism and Rationalism.* Amsterdam: Rodopi.

Nerlich, G. 1994. *The Shape of Space.* Cambridge: Cambridge University Press.

O'Connor, T. 2000. *Persons and Causes.* Oxford: Oxford University Press.

O'Hear, A. 1988. *The Element of Fire.* London: Routledge.

Pettit, P. 2001. *A Theory of Freedom: From the Psychology to the Politics of Agency.* Oxford: Oxford University Press.

Pettit, P., R. Sylvan & J. Norman (eds) 1987. *Metaphysics and Morality: Essays in Honour of J. J. C. Smart.* Oxford: Blackwell.

Place, U. T. 1996a. "'Intentionality as the Mark of Dispositional". *Dialectica* **50**: 91–120.

Place, U. T. 1996b. "Dispositions as Intentional States". In *Dispositions: A Debate,* D. M. Armstrong, C. B. Martin & U. T. Place (eds), 19–32. London: Routledge.

Place, U. T. 1999. "Intentionality and the Physical: A Reply to Mumford". *Philosophical Quarterly* **49**: 225–231.

Poincaré, H. 1952. *Science and Hypothesis.* New York: Dover.

Price, H. 1991. "Agency and Probabilistic Causality". *British Journal for the Philosophy of Science* **42**: 157–76.

Price, H. 1996. *Time's Arrow and Archimedes' Point.* Oxford: Oxford University Press.

Price, H. 2005. "Recent Work on the Arrow of Radiation". *Studies in the History and Philosophy of Modern Physics* **37**: 498–527.

Price, H. 2007. "Causal Perspectivalism". In *Causation, Physics and the Constitution of Reality,* H. Price & R. Corry (eds), 250–92. Oxford: Clarendon Press.

Prichard, H. A. [1937] 1949. "Moral Obligation". In his *Moral Obligation: Essays and Lectures,* 87–163. Oxford: Clarendon Press.

Prior, E. W., R. J. Pargetter & F. C. Jackson 1982. "Three Theses about Dispositions". *American Philosophical Quarterly* **19**: 251–7.

Putnam, H. 2005. "A Philosopher Looks at Quantum Mechanics (Again)". *British Journal for the Philosophy of Science* **56**: 615–34.

Quine, W. V. 1966. "The Scope and Language of Science". In his *Ways of Paradox and Other Essays,* 215–32. New York: Random House.

Rawls, J. 1972. *A Theory of Justice.* Oxford: Clarendon Press.

Reichenbach, H. 1956. *The Direction of Time.* Berkeley, CA: University of California Press.

Reichenbach, H. 1958. *The Philosophy of Space and Time,* M. Reichenbach & J. Freund (trans.). New York: Dover.

Salmon, W. C. 1984. *Scientific Explanation and the Causal Structure of the World.* Princeton, NJ: Princeton University Press.

Sankey, H. 2004. "Scientific Realism: An Elaboration and Defence". In *Knowledge and the World: Challenges Beyond the Science Wars,* M. Carrier, J. Roggenhofer, P. Blanchard & G. Küppers (eds), 55–74. Berlin: Springer.

Salmon, N. 1981. *Reference and Essence.* Princeton NJ: Princeton University Press.

Sayre-McCord, G. (ed.) 1988. *Essays on Moral Realism.* Ithaca, NY: Cornell University Press.

Scanlon, T. M. 1982. "Contractualism and Utilitarianism". In *Utilitarianism and Beyond*, A. Sen & B. Williams (eds), 103–28. Cambridge: Cambridge University Press.

Scanlon, T. M. 1998. *What We Owe to Each Other*. Cambridge, MA: Harvard University Press.

Searle, J. R. 2007. *Freedom and Neurobiology: Reflections on Free Will, Language and Political Power*. New York: Columbia University Press.

Shoemaker, S. 1980 "Causality and Properties". In *Time and Cause: Essays Presented to Richard Taylor*, P. van Inwagen (ed.), 109–35. Dordrecht: Reidel.

Shoemaker, S. 1998. "Causal and Metaphysical Necessity". *Pacific Philosophical Quarterly* **79**: 59–77.

Smart, J. J. C. 1957. "Critical Notice of H. Reichenbach's *The Direction of Time*". *Philosophical Quarterly* **8**: 72–7.

Smart, J. J. C. 1963. *Philosophy and Scientific Realism*. London: Routledge & Kegan Paul.

Smart, J. J. C. 1968. *Between Science and Philosophy*. New York: Random House.

Smart, J. J. C. 1973. "An Outline of a System of Utilitarian Ethics". In *Utilitarianism: For and Against*, J. J. C. Smart & B. Williams (eds). Cambridge: Cambridge University Press.

Smart, J. J. C. & B. Williams 1973. *Utilitarianism: For and Against*. Cambridge: Cambridge University Press.

Smith, H. 1991. "Deriving Morality from Rationality". In *Contractarianism and Rational Choice*, P. Vallentyne (ed.), 229–53. Cambridge: Cambridge University Press.

Smith, M. 1994. *The Moral Problem*. Oxford: Blackwell.

Swoyer, C. 1982. "The Nature of Natural Laws". *Australasian Journal of Philosophy* **60**: 203–23.

Strawson, G. 1986. *Freedom and Belief*. Oxford: Clarendon Press.

Vallentyne, P. (ed.) 1991. *Contractarianism and Rational Choice: Essays on David Gauthier's "Morals by Agreement"*. Cambridge: Cambridge University Press.

Van Fraassen, B. C. 1980. *The Scientific Image*. Oxford: Clarendon Press.

Van Fraassen, B. C. 1989. *Laws and Symmetry*. Oxford: Clarendon Press.

Watanabe, M. S. 1955. "Symmetry of Physical Laws. Part III, Prediction and Retrodiction". *Reviews of Modern Physics* **27**: 179–86.

Wichmann, E. H. 1971. *Berkeley Physics Course 4*. New York: McGraw-Hill.

Wilkerson, T. E. 1995. *Natural Kinds*. Aldershot: Ashgate.

Wong, D. B. 1984. *Moral Relativity*. Berkeley, CA: University of California Press.

Zeh, H. D. 2001. *The Physical Basis of the Direction of Time*, 4th edn. Berlin: Springer.

INDEX